Toward Understanding the Bible

Hermeneutics for Lay People

Perry B. Yoder

Faith and Life Press
Newton, Kansas

Library of Congress Catalog Card Number 78-53649
International Standard Book Number 0-87303-002-8

Printed in the United States of America

Design by John Hiebert
Printed by Mennonite Press, Inc.

Preface

In writing for a lay audience about a subject which is both sensitive (even controversial) and complex, it is difficult to find ways of saying things which are both accurate and advanced, yet understandable by those without specialized training. Whatever merits this work has along these lines is largely due to the efforts of two women. The first, a perceptive lay reader, Rose Martin, read an early draft of this work and filled the margins, backs of sheets, and even the spaces between the lines with most helpful comments. Out of this draft and her comments arose a major revision which served as a basis for this book. My debt to her shows throughout this work. The second is my wife, Elizabeth, who has tirelessly edited my opaque prose, challenged examples, and questioned the arrangement of material, until I am not sure whether this work is mine or hers. In addition, she has typed the several revisions through which this manuscript has gone. With such admirable help, what flaws yet exist in the present work are due to my own shortcomings.

I would also like to thank two churches in particular who gave me the opportunity to prepare some of this material for lay audiences—the Stirling Avenue Mennonite Church in Kitchener, Ontario, and the Oak Grove Mennonite Church near Wooster, Ohio. David Schroeder and Willard Swartley read the manuscript and suggested several helpful revisions. In addition there have been many individuals and churches along the way who have encouraged me, either by comment or by providing opportunity for discussion. May this work further facilitate the study and understanding of God's Word in the congregation.

Introduction

In the spring of 1975, my wife, Elizabeth, and I began a project which involved traveling throughout the Mennonite Church as itinerant Bible teachers. As we traveled and taught, we found that the issues that kept recurring usually came down, in the end, to what can be called the hermeneutical problem: How does one understand Scripture and how does one use it in today's situation? The decision to write an essay on the subject of hermeneutics for a lay audience arose out of that experience.

We became most aware of the problems of lay people in understanding and using Scripture as we studied with churches the Bible's teaching on male and female roles. For many, the simple quotation of a few isolated references from Paul's writings was not satisfying. Most sincere Bible users seemed uncomfortable with such a "proof-texting" approach, yet any interpretation which seemed to counter the plain sense of these references was also regarded with suspicion. "Explaining" a text, at times, was felt to come close to "explaining it away." Thus arose a dilemma for many. While a few key texts from Paul were no longer regarded as sufficient *alone* to guide the practice of the church, they still exercised considerable influence, as well they should.

We found that the most helpful way to begin the study of Paul's teaching on women was to begin with a brief analysis of how one understands and uses the Bible generally. After a discussion of some general hermeneutical principles, not only did Pauline material about women become better understood, but its relevancy for today could become apparent. The present work, in fact, owes its origin to these introductory sketches. (This will also explain the frequent use of passages in Paul dealing with women for purposes of illustration.) But beyond the problem of male and female relationships, this work is offered in the hope that it will help those seeking biblical answers for today's problems to find a coherent and consistent way of using the biblical text.

Another problem we saw in our travel arose from the tremendous bombardment of our churches and homes with religious publications of every kind. This material varies greatly in quality as well as in viewpoint, but the average layperson seemed to accept this diversity quite easily. We saw a great deal of what might be considered "bad consumerism" of religious materials. For example, books on prophecy by popular writers are often used by discussion groups. These groups become caught up in the viewpoint of the book without any real testing of what is being said. Rarely are Scripture references checked to see if they really mean what the author claims. Even more rarely are other works on the same topic read to gain the perspective of another viewpoint. The attitude seems to be, If a sincere person wrote it, it must be true. The result of this is that people feel free to pick and choose what suits them. All too often the result is a cop-out—people latch onto a strain of Christianity that affirms them where they are. The Bible becomes a defender of the status quo rather than an agent of growth.

This lack of concern with a rigorous study or tough-minded understanding of Scripture has both fed and been influenced by the "charismatic" movement, where the journey has been inward with an emphasis on individual experience. In such a climate the temptation at times becomes almost irresistible either to grant ultimate authority to personal experience and insight or to assume that the meaning of Scripture is somehow directly mediated almost without the aid of human understanding. In such cases it is easy to mistake personal opinion for understanding, one's own reasoning for divine guidance. Instead, I believe a careful and accurate study of Scripture is necessary to escape this subjective individualism. Indeed, the rigorous study of the Bible which leads to real understanding is the best way we have of allowing the Spirit to guide us.

Even more influential than these competing religious voices are the influences of secular society on the church. Change itself is inevitable. The question for Christian people is, Can we change without losing our Christian identity and its authentic expression in life? I believe the answer to this question lies in whether we will be able to use the Bible as a rudder in the midst of change, rather than as a club to resist change. If we succeed in doing the former, we will maintain our identity as Christian people who live in faithful obedience—but expressing this in ever new ways. If we do the latter, we will change nevertheless, but erratically, often in damaging ways. In the end, the Bible itself will become less credible because of the uses to which we put it.

A third series of problems and issues arose from the gap that naturally exists between how the layperson reads the Bible and how the scholar studies it. Since in my "real" life I am a college Bible teacher, churches sometimes wanted me to explain how scholars study the Bible and what relevancy this might have for local congregations. Usually the response to such a presentation was, "Well, lay people could never do that," or "Those presuppositions might be fine for scholars, but they are hardly necessary for us 'regular' folk." This tendency to brush off biblical scholarship as irrelevant or as, perhaps, even detrimental to the spiritual life of believers and congregations is troubling to me personally. First of all, it may represent a misunderstanding of the various ways in which the Bible can be used. But secondly, and more importantly, if there is going to be real dialogue between scholar and church, there will need to be some common agreement about how one studies the Bible, regardless of level or intensity of understanding. I am convinced that the Bible will continue to influence the church and guide it, if it is not only handled reverently, but also studied and used in ways which make sense. The third purpose, then, of the present work, is to begin to lay the foundation for the basic assumptions about the study of the Bible which can be shared by lay people and scholar alike.

One final note regarding that formidable word *hermeneutics,* which has already been used several times in this introduction, and a related term, *exegesis,* which is not much better known by lay people. Exegesis is the study of a particular text in the Bible (or in any literature for that matter). The goal of exegesis is simply to explain or bring out the meaning of the text. Since in trying to draw out the meaning of a text, different techniques, such as word study, study of the historical background, etc., must be used, exegesis is also very concerned with method—that is, with *how* we should study a text to find its meaning. Though most people who read the Bible do not use the term *exegesis,* there is nothing particularly mysterious about it—most people, in fact, practice some form of exegesis whenever they study the Bible. They try to get the gist or meaning of a passage and they usually have a certain way of going about it.

Hermeneutics, on the other hand, is not so interested in the specific explanation of individual passages, but in a more general way with the object or goal of exegesis. If in exegesis the aim is to discover the meaning of a passage, how will we tell when we have gotten this? In this essay we see that the task of hermeneutics is to teach us how we may tell a valid explanation from an invalid one—what constitutes a correct understanding of a passage. Again, this is not something different from what we do all the time when we sort out likely explanations from those that are less likely. But hermeneutics is not only interested in deciding what is a valid interpretation; it is also concerned with how interpretations are used—how we may apply our understanding of Scripture to the problems of our life today. Thus hermeneutics is the more comprehensive term. While exegesis may be considered the nitty-gritty of constructing interpretations, hermeneutics deals with their validation and application.[1]

Because we are more interested, in this work, with the process of understanding—hermeneutics—than with setting forth "correct" examples of exegesis, we will often not give a full explanation of a text. Instead we will sketch the kind of questions which must be answered for a correct understanding to take place. We will point out the route rather than describe the goal minutely. Hopefully this will not be too disconcerting. We intend for the reader to focus on what, in general, represents a correct understanding, rather than to debate specific interpretations of individual texts. It is our wish in those cases where controversial passages are treated, that the discussion will not be sidetracked by becoming too involved in the particulars of the passage itself.

Footnotes

[1] Hermeneutics has been defined in two basically different ways. On the one hand, as here, it is seen as explaining "what it means to understand"—focusing on both the goal and the validation of understanding. Seen this way, the task is to explain or suggest the prerequisites for understanding. The assumption is that understanding takes place constantly as we speak and write; what is needed is to lay bare the ingredients of this process.

On the other hand, some see hermeneutics as a philosophy of understanding: Is it possible for understanding to take place? Can we really understand another? These questions have not been dealt with at any length here, since this is not the task of hermeneutics as envisioned in this work.

Related to this problem in the philosophy of understanding is the problem of how words "mean" as discussed by philosophers of language. Again, how words actually do mean is not discussed here—our basic assumption is that words do mean (e.g., communicate) and our task is to understand this as best we can. In short, this work is written for the reader or listener—the one confronted by linguistic data—in order to enable him to better understand what he is reading or hearing. Our specific focus is the Bible—how the lay reader may read with greater understanding and decide between the conflicting interpretations of others. This is not a philosophical analysis of either how this is possible or how linguistic data can mean.

Contents

PART I | Getting It Straight

". . . There's glory for you!" (said Humpty Dumpty.)

"I don't know what you mean by 'glory,' " Alice said.

Humpty Dumpty smiled contemptuously. "Of course you don't—till I tell you. I meant 'there's a nice knock-down argument for you!' "

"But 'glory' doesn't mean a 'nice knock-down argument,' " Alice objected.

"When I use the word," Humpty Dumpty said, in rather a scornful tone, "it means just what I choose it to mean—neither more nor less."

"The question is," said Alice, "whether you can make words mean so many different things."

"The question is," said Humpty Dumpty, "which is to be master—that's all."

Lewis Carroll, Through the Looking Glass

1 | Games People Play with the Bible

1.1 *Interpretational games*

G. Irvin Lehman, who has been for many years a teacher at Eastern Mennonite Seminary, is reported to have said on occasion in his Bible classes, "Everyone thinks they take the Bible as it stands, but in reality they take it as they understand it." This pithy saying points to two basic facts about the understanding of the Bible today. The first is that all who hold the Bible dear, who use it as a basis for faith and life, claim to be taking the Bible as it is. No one is trying to deliberately misunderstand the Bible. Yet, there seem to be as many understandings of Scripture as there are readers. Many indeed claim that only their understanding is correct, while others must be faulty.

Part—but only part—of this babel of conflicting interpretations stems from people not all using the same ground rules when they set out to understand Scripture. In studying Scripture, a variety of interpretational games are being played, all with their special rules. Given this diversity of rules and games, a variety of conflicting understandings is inevitable. In this chapter we want to describe a number of these games, ending with an alternative that, for reasons to be described in detail in later sections, is the most productive for the real understanding of Scripture.

1.2 *The Author Game*

Perhaps the most common game played in Bible study is the "Author Game." In this game the words of the Bible are a passive "it" and the modern reader is the active force which breathes meaning into them. This game usually begins with one of the following openings: "The meaning I found here. . ."; "To me, this passage means. . ."; "I find this idea meaningful. . . ." Notice the use of the first person pronoun, *I* or *me*. The individual reader has become the author, using the Bible to sponsor that person's own meaning and understanding. Actually, of course, the words in the Bible were written by real people who had something to say.

When we play author, we short-circuit the text—substituting our meaning for theirs. To be sure, we want to get something meaningful out of the Bible, but we must be sure to get out what the authors put in, not our own contribution.

The Author Game is played in part because people so easily slip into a false notion of the relationship between thought and reality. If people playing the Author Game were challenged, they might respond by saying that they think this is the meaning which the author wished to communicate. If asked why, they might say, "It seems logical to me," or "It makes sense to me." As a matter of fact, however, what seems logical to me—what makes sense to me—and what is actually the case, may be two entirely different things.

Two men were driving along a prairie highway in Kansas. The driver of the car was from Kansas, while his passenger was from a mountain town in Colorado. The weather was stormy and the wind was blowing. Snow was beginning to fall. Suddenly a grayish white object rolled into their path. The driver steered resolutely on, while the passenger tried to twist the steering wheel from his grasp to avoid the object. The car hit the rolling ball without apparent effect, as the driver from Kansas expected. He knew it was a tumbleweed. His passenger from Colorado perceived it as a boulder, since from his experience this is what usually goes rolling across roads. The fact that we think something is so does not make it so. We need something besides our own opinions or experiences to justify an interpretation.

The major flaw in the Author Game is that it begins at the wrong end, with us thinking our thoughts into the text as if this made it so, rather than with the reality that lies in, around, and behind the text. It is at the latter end that we must begin if we would achieve an authentic understanding of the text.

1.3 *The Pope Game*

Sometimes those who play the Author Game—especially when it is pointed out what they are doing—go on to play the "Pope Game." In the Pope Game we have the infallible opinion. To play this game successfully one justifies an interpretation by an appeal to some source or basis which is not open to either objection or inspection. Phrases like "If I'm sincere . . .," or "If I just believe. . .," or "The Holy Spirit will show me. . ." usually begin this game. The problem with this game is its lack of both logic and common sense. Logically, there is a difference between *believing* that something is right and its actually *being* right. The action of believing does not make something that is incorrect, correct. Likewise, common sense tells us that sincerity is no evidence of a correct understanding. There have always been misguided, sadly mistaken, but sincere, zealots.

The same is true of invoking the Holy Spirit. The Holy Spirit may be *necessary* to a Christian understanding of Scripture, but the Holy Spirit is not *sufficient* to guarantee a correct understanding. Many differences in interpretation that we face today are differences promoted by people who claim to have the Holy Spirit and feel that the Holy Spirit guarantees the correctness of their own particular understanding. This in part explains why in conservative circles the debate over differing interpretations is often so bitter. Since these people are relying on the Holy Spirit, they must be right and all others wrong. The sad fact is, they are playing a futile game—relying on the Holy Spirit does not guarantee a correct understanding of Scripture. Compounding this, the Author Game is often simultaneously being played, so that their use of the Bible's words to author their own meaning is given authority in the name of the Holy Spirit—thus, the infallible opinion.

1.4 *The Caveman Game*

Another game is the "Caveman Game." In this game, one begins with several Scriptures which are used to "prove" something. Then, having established this base, it is used as a club a la caveman against all other opinions, interpretations, and ideas. The people who play this game can be recognized by their unwillingness to grapple seriously with Scriptures which seem contrary to their own views. They have found the magic key to Scripture and use it to subdue all others. This game is a defensive one as well. By standing firmly on their own (narrow) base, they can resist all thoughtful consideration of other positions, they can insure themselves of learning nothing unless it agrees with what they already hold true, and in the end they can be sure that they will never need to change their minds (come out of their cave, so to speak).

1.5 *The Born Again Game*

Many people, however, rather than playing Caveman, rely on the "Born Again Game." In this game the trick is to mistake the beginning of the Christian life for the goal. The game usually begins with a story—how some person reading the Bible all by himself became a Christian. The implication is that all one really needs to do is read the Bible and the rest is clear. It's only when study begins that troubles arise. The fallacy of this game is to mistake the level of understanding which leads to becoming a Christian with the level of understanding which leads to Christian growth and maturity. The Christian life can be likened to the growth of an infant into an adult. We feed infants milk, but as they grow we begin to feed them solids, until they can handle an adult diet. The Bible must not be mistaken as being only milk for infants. For it to be meat, we need to advance beyond the Born Again Game and its level of understanding (1 Cor. 3:1, 2).

A variant of this game is "The Priesthood of All Believers Game." The rules of this game are that since the Bible is understandable by all lay people, no higher level of understanding is needed. In fact, to promote knowledge above this lowest common denominator is somehow an attack on the laity. This game is based on a mistaken notion of the church, for in reality there are many special gifts—knowledge included—which are not shared equally by all Christians. These gifts are given, however, for the nourishment of the body of Christ, so that all Christians may grow in spiritual maturity as a result of these special gifts (1 Cor. 12, Eph. 4:4-16). Thus, differences in knowledge are necessary for growth, rather than a threat to the church. In fact, growth and prosperity in knowledge should be supported and encouraged by the church.

1.6 *The Literal Game*

Related to all the games above is the "Literal Game." The creed of this game is "I take the Bible literally." Usually accompanying this is some disclaimer such as, "I'm just a simple layperson, so. . .," or "We should just read the Bible as it is and not try to explain it away." The fallacy of this game is that this slogan hides what is really happening. In reality, what is presented as the "literal meaning" is the interpretation chosen by the person himself, not the meaning that the passage must have.

One morning our five-year-old son's memory verse in Sunday school was ". . . We must obey God, rather than men" (Acts 5:29). After Sunday school, his teacher reported to us that his response to the verse was, "Oh, now I know that I don't need to obey Daddy, but I do need to obey Mamma!" Now what could be more literal? He needed to know yet that the word *men* doesn't only mean males but can also mean people—both male and female. His obvious reply to this explanation would be, "Oh, goody, now I don't need to obey either Dad or Mom!" If it were explained to him that *men* in this verse meant "rulers" and the verse doesn't have anything to do with obeying Mama and Daddy, he might reply, "Well, I'm just a simple child, and I like to take the Bible as it is written. This saying 'men' means 'rulers' sounds like trying to explain the text away. If it means 'rulers,' why doesn't it just say 'rulers'? I'll stick with my literal interpretation: I'm not supposed to obey men—Daddy included." From this partly hypothetical story we can see the myth of the literal interpretation. Words don't mean just one thing; they mean a variety of things in a variety of situations. We are mistaking myth for reality when we choose one meaning and, by calling it "literal," declare it correct and undebatable.

Not only does the Literal Game reflect misunderstanding about language, but by necessity it leads to a pick-and-choose use of Scripture, because a literal interpretation cannot be applied consistently to the same type of language. For example, we have Paul's injunction in

1 Corinthians 14:34, "The women should keep silence in the churches" (RSV), or in Romans 13:1, "Let every person be subject to the governing authorities" (RSV). Many plead that we should be literally obedient to such commands. Yet the same persons would not call for literal obedience to teachings of Jesus such as these: "So therefore, whoever of you does not renounce all that he has cannot be my disciple" (Lk. 14:33, RSV), or "Sell your possessions, and give alms" (Lk. 12:33a, RSV). A principle of interpretation which must be applied inconsistently is obviously not to be trusted. Rather than helping the Bible speak to us, this method uses the Bible to defend presently held beliefs and assumptions, while ignoring the Bible where it would challenge these. So-called literal interpretation with its pick-and-choose hermeneutic is in reality often a way of suppressing the Bible.

With so many different interpretational games being played, it is not surprising that people often become suspicious of the validity of any interpretation. Interpretation for many comes close to being a synonym for opinion, as in the expression "Well, that's your interpretation." In such a state of affairs, interpretations are chosen on the basis of one's own opinion. If the result of someone else's study agrees with us, then it must be right; if it doesn't, we feel free to reject it. The classic phrase representing this point of view is "He comes out at the right place." But this is putting the cart before the horse—placing our preconceived conclusions about what the Bible must say before a careful consideration of what it does say. On the contrary, it is not where a person comes out, but how he got there that shows the correctness of his results. The kind of game played determines the kind of results gotten and their value.

1.7 Game-free Bible Study

The problem with all of the games described above is that they do not teach us what we don't already know nor challenge us to do differently than we already do. Playing them, we do not discover someone else talking, but hear only ourselves. The Bible becomes a launching pad for our ideas, rather than a source of new ideas.

But how can we become "honest" readers? We must begin by learning game-free Bible study—study based on proper rules for understanding. In order to free ourselves from gamesmanship with the Bible, we need to become clear about what it takes to enter into a dialogue with the author, what is needed on our part. Correct understanding means not only giving up the wrong games, but developing, positively, an approach on our part which will lead to understanding, so that when we find new conclusions and old ones challenged, we can be assured of the correctness of our new understandings. As a first step in learning game-free Bible study which preserves the integrity of the biblical text, we must understand how language works, what happens when people express themselves.

In normal language, it is the writer or speaker who uses language to "say" something. We, the audience, understand when we realize what it is that the speaker intends for us to comprehend. The speaker is the donor; the audience, the recipient, as in the following diagram:

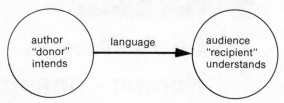

The two circles in the diagram represent the two parties needed for communication: a source, the author; and a receiver, the audience. Language bridges the gap between them, flowing from the donor to the recipient, as indicated by the arrows. The audience, in its role as receiver, is not passive but active—its action is directed toward trying to understand the author. What too often happens in reading the Bible, however, is that the language is short-circuited like this:

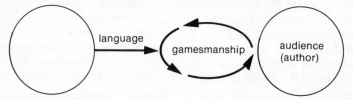

We, the audience, play our games, and the biblical words become the board for our gamesmanship. The author is a blank—he is ignored in these games. Common sense tells us this isn't the way to understand another person. These games, in fact, short-circuit the whole process of communication. On the contrary, the "golden rule" on which honest understanding is based takes the author and his language seriously: Understand another's words as he wants them to be understood, not as we want to understand them.[1] We observe this golden rule of understanding when we try inductively to discover what an author meant by the words he used. This is game-free Bible study.

Footnotes
1. The idea of a golden rule of interpretation I take from E. D. Hirsch, *The Aims of Interpretation* (Chicago: University of Chicago Press, 1976), p. 90-91. He writes, *"Unless there is a powerful overriding value in disregarding an author's intention (i.e., original meaning), we. . . should not disregard it . . . .* When we simply use an author's words for our own purposes without respecting his intention, we transgress what Charles Stevenson in another context called 'the ethics of language,' just as we transgress ethical norms when we use another person merely for our own ends."

2 | The Bible: God's Word in Human Language

2.1 *The Bible as Normal Human Language*

As we saw in the previous chapter, to understand the Bible we must give up our games and approach its understanding sensibly, as we would approach any human language. But the Bible is not like any other book— it is the Word of God, a divine revelation. How can a commonsense approach to understanding language be of help in understanding the Bible? Is not the Bible's language to be understood differently than other language?

The fact is that the language of the Bible is human language like that found in any ordinary book and must be understood in the same way. The difference between the Bible and an ordinary book is that the *content* that is being communicated is vastly more important. It is, indeed, the Word of God, and as such has far more influence and claim on us than does any other book. But the *way* we understand the words (the content) which are communicated is no different from the way we understand the words of Shakespeare or Milton.

This may sound like a very shocking statement. How can one compare the language in the Bible with any other language? But those who have thought about studying and understanding the Bible see that indeed it is exactly this that must be done. No special language was created in which to write the Bible. The Bible was written in human languages, mainly Hebrew and Greek, which were used for ordinary secular communication. Furthermore, the Greek and Hebrew language which we find in the Bible is to be understood exactly in the same way as the Greek and Hebrew that we find outside of the Bible.

This principle has been affirmed over and over by interpreters of many theological perspectives. For example, Warfield, a conservative scholar of the last century, wrote, "And the Holy Ghost in using human speech, used it as he found it. . . . The current sense of a phrase is alone to be considered, and if men so spoke and were understood correctly in so speaking, the Holy Ghost, speaking their speech would also so speak."[1] Here Warfield stresses that the Holy Spirit used the normal, natural conventions of the language at the time the Bible was written to give expression to revelation. Indeed, it is the fact that the Bible is written in normal human language that makes it possible for us to understand it. As William J. Martin states, "The language of the Bible shares all the characteristics of human language; if it had been otherwise, it would have been incomprehensible to us."[2]

Likewise, Ryrie, dean of Dallas Theological Seminary, a conservative dispensationalist, has written, "The Scriptures, then, cannot be regarded as an illustration of some special use of language so that in the interpretation of these Scriptures some deeper meaning of the words must be sought."[3] As these conservative—even fundamentalist— scholars recognize, the methods and techniques necessary for understanding ordinary language will also be necessary for understanding the Bible, since it too was written in normal language, used in normal ways and communicating meaning like all human language.

2.2 Evidence of Human Authorship

The fact that God chose to be revealed through human language, as written by human beings, shows that God saw human language as an adequate mode for His revelation. God indeed seems to have taken human authorship seriously, not turning people into dictating machines, but letting each write with his own style and from his own perspective. The Gospel of John, for example, is quite different from the other three Gospels. John's vocabulary is distinctive, stylized terms like *truth* and *light* occurring frequently. In John's Gospel, Jesus tells no parables, but instead speaks in long discourses. John's grammar is perhaps the simplest in the New Testament. In fact, beginning Greek students traditionally start reading the New Testament with the Gospel of John and are then frustrated by the difficulty of the material when they begin reading another Gospel such as Luke, whose style is much more complex.

While the obvious and extensive differences in style and perspective in the different books of the Bible show plainly that God used particular individual human agents to communicate His revelation, there are also a number of other factors that point in the same direction. In Paul's letters, for example, we can see many signs of Paul's own thinking and involvement in writing. In I Corinthians 4:19, he writes, "If the Lord is willing, however, I will come to you soon," while in 16:5-9 he implies that there may be some delay in his coming. These references look like a man trying to make travel plans, which change as his circumstances change. If these were directly dictated by God, why not just say he was going to come—certainly God would not need to say "if the Lord is willing."

This immediate personal involvement of Paul in his writings is further illustrated in his letter to the Corinthians where he writes:

I thank God that I did not baptize any of you except Crispus and Gaius. No one can say, then, that you were baptized as my disciples. (Oh, yes, I also baptized Stephanus and his family; but I can't remember whether I baptized anyone else) (1 Cor. 1:14-16, TEV).

Here we see Paul making a statement to support his main point which he then, upon further thought (perhaps as he reread the letter), must modify, ending up finally by confessing that he doesn't quite remember. This looks for all the world like a man at first writing passionately to make a point, and then remembering more details about which he is not quite clear.

On numerous occasions as above, Paul used the personal pronoun I— "I am sure that. . ." (Phil. 1:6), "my opinion. . ." (2 Cor. 8:10), etc. Again, we get the picture of one who is consciously writing from his own perspective, in his own words.

Furthermore, a biblical writer, like the writer of any book, might do careful research to get the facts straight before writing. For example, in the beginning of the Gospel of Luke we find the following statement:

Many people have done their best to write a report of the things that have taken place among us. They wrote what we have been told by those who saw these things from the beginning and who proclaimed the message. And so, Your Excellency, because I have carefully studied all these matters from their beginning, I thought it would be good to write an orderly account for you (Lk. 1:1-3, TEV).

This is clearly a picture of a man who has done careful research and now, having thought about these things at length, is trying to set forth, as best he can, an orderly account. Again, the activity and agency of the human author is obvious and striking.

Because of these differences in style, vocabulary, and thought from writer to writer in the Bible, it is clear that the words and expressions of Scripture reflect the minds and language of particular men even though inspired by God. Thus, when we refer to the author or writer, we mean the immediate human author who actually penned the words.

2.3 *The Bible and the Incarnation*

An analogy to this fact of divine revelation coming through the medium of human language is the Incarnation. God took upon Himself the form of a man in Jesus, and this had similar implications. Philippians 2:7 tells how He "emptied himself" of His divinity, "taking the form of a bond-servant." He was now limited by the human form He took, or else *empty* and *take on* would be hollow terms. As a man He suffered as men do. When He stubbed his toe, it hurt; when the sun shone in His eyes, He squinted. Likewise, the fact that the Word of God comes to us clothed in the words of men means it too is subject to both the limitations and the possibilities of human language.

Now this matter of having the divine in human form has always been felt by some to be a bit offensive. The constant tendency has been to magnify Jesus' deity and to play down His humanity. Thus, from the very beginning the church has had to safeguard the humanity of Jesus in its creeds and teachings. Likewise, the fact that God's revelation has come through human language makes some people uncomfortable. Consequently, doctrines have been erected to "safeguard" revelation from any human "contamination." (In some ways this is reminiscent of the Catholic church's attempt to safeguard the deity of Jesus by providing a doctrine of the special nature of His mother—the Immaculate Conception.) If God was willing to take human authors and language seriously enough to reveal Himself in and through them, we must be at least as willing to do so too.

2.4 *The Nature of the Bible and Understanding*

The point that should not be overlooked is that even if such doctrines as a divine dictation theory were accepted, they would not guarantee a correct understanding of Scripture. Arguments about the nature of the Bible are actually a red herring in discussions of how to understand the Bible, since a little reflection will show that in fact doctrines of inspiration, revelation, etc., do not solve the problem of understanding the Bible. This is because these doctrines concern the *nature* of the Bible, not our understanding of it. Now, this point is often overlooked by those who devote their energies to such matters. They often assume that if the character of the Bible is defined, then the battle is won. On the contrary, the whole doctrine of inspiration comes to no avail if we do not correctly understand the inspired text!

This oversight leads to another futile game that is played with the Bible—arguing about the nature of the Bible as if this were the same as understanding the Bible. Francis Schaeffer, for example, writes, "The question is a simple one when viewed from the whole cultural and intellectual spectrum. It is: In the Bible do we have propositional revelation which gives us knowledge which we cannot have from ourselves beginning from ourselves, or do we not?"[4] Even granted his proposition (Author Game?) that the Bible's revelation is in the form of propositional revelation, the far from simple question is, How do we gain understanding of this? All these divine propositions may be misunderstood! The question really is, in Schaeffer's terms, not, *Do* we have propositional revelation, but, How can we have valid knowledge of them?

As Beegle writes in his recent treatment of inspiration and revelation, "The most pressing problem of Christians is not a correct view of inspiration, but a correct method of interpreting the canon."[5]

We know from experience that neither a "high" view of Scripture nor the presence of the Holy Spirit in life keeps people from false interpretations. From history we can learn that interpretations regarded as valid fifty or one hundred years ago are no longer considered correct. Likewise today, dispensationalists who agree in adhering to verbal plenary inspiration, disagree in their understanding and interpretation of Scripture. For example, there is wide disagreement on such fundamental points as when the present dispensation began or when it will end. In sum, doctrines on the nature of the Bible will not solve the problem of how we can understand the text. These, in fact, often serve as a cloak for a gamesmanship approach to the Bible.

2.5 *Summary*

To return to the point at which we started this discussion, the fact that God's revelation comes through human language does not alter the fact of its being human language. Thus all games which are either contrary to or which short-circuit the golden rule of understanding, form a shaky basis for understanding Scripture. What we understand in the Bible may be unique in its power, authority, or content, but the way we understand it is in common with all human language. The solution to the problem of understanding the Bible is not, then, more "orthodox" doctrines of inspiration and revelation, nor a greater presence of the Holy Spirit (although these may help), but a better grasp of how to understand. As Beegle has written, "Not all understandings of the Bible are equally valid, and so the basic criterion for determining God's truth is the proper use of reason working with all the available data."[6] Our present task, then, is to find a rational inductive way to understand language and test the validity of competing interpretations.

Footnotes
1. *Inspiration and Authority of the Bible,* p. 438, quoted in John Beekman and John Callow, *Translating the Word of God* (Grand Rapids, Mich.: Zondervan, 1974), p. 346.
2. William J. Martin, "Special Revelation as Objective," in *Revelation and the Bible,* ed., Carl F. Henry (Grand Rapids, Mich.: Baker Book House, 1967), p. 70.
3. Charles C. Ryrie, *Dispensationalism Today* (Chicago: Moody Press, 1973), p. 70.
4. Francis Schaeffer, "Letters to the Editor," *The Other Side,* September-October 1976, p.6.
5. Dewey M. Beegle, *Scripture, Tradition and Infallibility* (Grand Rapids, Mich.: Eerdmans, 1973), p. 263.
6. *Ibid.,* p. 302.

PART II | How Language Works

The table was a large one, but the three were all crowded together at one corner of it. "No room! No room!" they cried out when they saw Alice coming. "There's plenty of room!" said Alice indignantly, and she sat down in a large arm-chair at one end of the table.

"Have some wine," the March Hare said in an encouraging tone.

Alice looked all round the table, but there was nothing on it but tea. "I don't see any wine," she remarked.

"There isn't any," said the March Hare.

"Then it wasn't very civil of you to offer it," said Alice angrily.

"It wasn't very civil of you to sit down without being invited," said the March Hare.

"I didn't know it was your table," said Alice: "It's laid for a great many more than three."

"Your hair wants cutting," said the Hatter. He had been

looking at Alice for some time with great curiosity, and this was his first speech.

"You should learn not to make personal remarks," Alice said with some severity: "It's very rude."

The Hatter opened his eyes very wide on hearing this; but all he said was, "Why is a raven like a writing-desk?"

"Come, we shall have some fun now!" thought Alice. "I'm glad they've begun asking riddles—I believe I can guess that," she added aloud.

"Do you mean that you think you can find out the answer to it?" said the March Hare.

"Exactly so," said Alice.

"Then you should say what you mean," the March Hare went on.

"I do," Alice hastily replied; "at least—at least I mean what I say—that's the same thing, you know."

"Not the same thing a bit!" said the Hatter. "Why, you might just as well say that 'I see what I eat' is the same thing as 'I eat what I see'!"

"You might as well say," added the March Hare, "that 'I like what I get' is the same thing as 'I get what I like'!"

"You might just as well say," added the Dormouse, which seemed to be talking in its sleep, "that 'I breathe when I sleep' is the same thing as 'I sleep when I breathe'!"

"It is the same thing with you," said the Hatter, and here the conversation dropped. . . .

Lewis Carroll, Alice's Adventures in Wonderland

3 | How Language Works

3.1 *Says and Means*

An angel of the Lord said to Philip, "Get ready and go south to the road that goes from Jerusalem to Gaza." . . . So Philip got ready and went. Now an Ethiopian eunuch, who was an important official in charge of the treasury of the queen of Ethiopia, was on his way home. He had been to Jerusalem to worship God and was going back home in his carriage. As he rode along, he was reading from the book of the prophet Isaiah. The Holy Spirit said to Philip, "Go over to the carriage and stay close to it." Philip ran over and heard him reading from the book of the prophet Isaiah. He asked him, *"Do you understand what you are reading*?"

The official replied, "How can I understand unless someone explains it to me?" And he invited Philip to climb up and sit in the carriage with him (Acts 8:26-31, TEV).

This story illustrates a basic feature of language—there is a difference between what is *said* and what is *meant.* The problem of the Ethiopian official was not that he could not read—as an educated person he knew well enough what the passage said. His problem was that he did not know what it meant. To determine the meaning, he needed an explanation.

We can see from this example that *to know what something says is not necessarily to understand what it means.* But how often we overlook this basic fact of language when we read the Bible. We usually assume that to hear or read what the Bible *says* is to automatically understand what it *means.* Many times we hear ourselves say, "The Bible says. . .," just as if it were perfectly evident from quoting a passage what it means. On the contrary, the distinction between what is said and what is meant is rooted in the very nature of language itself. Linguists refer to this aspect of language as "duality."[1]

3.2 *Duality*

We can understand duality in language best by comparing language with other kinds of communication systems. For example, when we see a red traffic light, we know that this means stop, while a green light means go. There is a one-to-one correspondence between the sign and meaning—red never means anything else, and no other color means stop. The signal, we can say, "carries" or "has" meaning. In this type of communication system there is no ambiguity.

Now, in language there is no such correlation between symbol and meaning. At all levels of language there is a difference between sound and meaning. For example, at the level of individual sounds, this is quite obvious. In the word *bats* the *s* sound can have at least three meanings. It can mean the plural—several bats; it can be the possessive—the bat's cave; or it can signify third person singular, present tense verb—the boy bats the ball. We have here no simple correlation between sound and meaning. Likewise, the same meaning can be communicated by several different sounds. The idea of plural is expressed in English by the sound *s* in bats, but by the sound *z* in dogs and by the sound *iz* in bosses. (Although all these words end in *s*, if you pronounce them you can hear different sounds.) Because of this lack of congruence between sound and meaning, the sound *s* is ambiguous—it has a variety of possible meanings.

Things are no different at the level of words. The same word (a series of sounds) can mean quite different things. The word *sail* can mean the action of sailing (verb) or the object that makes a boat go before the wind (noun). Likewise, the same meaning can be expressed by different words—*bachelor* and *unmarried man,* for example. Again, since there is no close correlation between symbol and meaning, ambiguity is built into language.

Even at the level of the sentence we find this ambiguity. For instance, the statement "The shooting of the soldiers frightened me" has at least two different meanings: (1) "When the soldiers were shot, I was frightened," or (2) "When the soldiers shot, I was frightened." The "says" is the same, but either meaning could legitimately be borne by it. This aspect of language—dualism—means that on the one hand there is a system of sounds, words, and sentences, and on the other, the meaning which these express. Since there is no one-to-one correspondence between the two, we must say that *words do not have meaning, but are used to express or convey meaning. Because of this, there is always a difference between what is said or written and what is meant.*

This built-in ambiguity is one reason why the idea that a "literal interpretation" is true, is wrong. (See 1.5.) If words "had" meaning it could be true—but they do not. Thus language is necessarily ambiguous. Only in communication systems where there is no ambiguity can there be true literal interpretation. A red light can 'literally' mean stop, but 'sail' does not have a *literal* meaning—it has a variety of *possible* meanings.

Translators have long recognized this fundamental fact of dualism. Indeed, if it were not so, the translation of an author's thoughts would be impossible. If meaning could only be expressed by certain specific words (sounds), then translating the meaning into other languages would be impossible, because different words (sounds) would need to be used. We would all need to learn Hebrew and Greek to get the Bible's meaning, since these were the specific words in which the meaning was expressed. But as soon as we recognize the legitimacy of translation, then we must also recognize that the same meaning can be expressed in a variety of words, and that there is no absolute correlation between what is meant and what is said.

Translators realize that to literally translate word by word what is said, in fact changes the meaning. For example, to translate Mark 10:38, "Can you drink the cup of suffering that I must drink?" word for word into the language of a certain South American tribe would mean that Jesus is challenging James and John to a drinking contest![2] Again, what is meant is one thing; how it is expressed or said is another. We cannot automatically go from what is said to what is meant.

3.3 *Duality and Intention*

This difference between what is said and what is meant in language helps us to see more clearly what is involved in understanding. Since words and sentences may have a variety of legitimate meanings, how do we know what is the *actual* meaning in a sentence or passage which we are studying? Since ambiguity is built into language, how can we know what is actually meant? To discover this, we must go back to the author who used certain words to express something. When someone uses words, that person has a particular sense of the word in view. Thus the act of using words is to use them in a certain actual sense—to assign them a particular meaning. It is our task, then, as audience, to determine what sense the author wished his or her words to have. We do this through uncovering the intentions behind the use of words. From our estimate of the author's intentions we then make judgments about the meanings the words are to have in a particular instance. This is the word's *actual* meaning. For example, in the illustration discussed earlier, we can see that in the phrase "We ought to obey God rather than men" the word *men* could *possibly* mean (1) people, both male and female; (2) males; (3) rulers. This is to say, the word does not have a meaning, but rather is ambiguous. But in its context, as spoken by Peter, it *actually* means "rulers." We understand the word *men* to mean this because of our judgment about what Peter intends to communicate in this particular situation by his use of the word *men*. (Remember the golden rule of understanding.) The following diagram will help to clarify this:

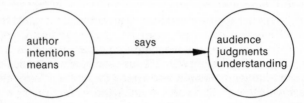

If we want to understand someone, we must begin with what is said, and then determine what is meant. We do this by overcoming the chasm between the author and audience through building a bridge from what is said to what is meant, using judgments about the author's intentions as the foundation. Indeed, since every act of understanding must bridge this gap between says and means, *a judgment about the intentions lying behind a statement is a necessary part of understanding all language.*

Perhaps an analogy from another area of human activity will illustrate the essential importance of this estimate of intentions for understanding. A group of men go deer hunting together. During the course of the day they become separated from each other. Suddenly one of the hunters sees a deer, aims, and fires. But instead of hitting the deer, he kills one of his fellow hunters. An inquest is held concerning the death. Is this a case of accidental homicide, or is it a case of murder? What happened in either case is the same; the only difference is how we understand what happened. How we understand what happened depends in turn on our understanding of the intentions of the one who shot his fellow hunter. If we know that this was his first hunt, that he was not a particularly good shot, and that the man who was killed was one of his best friends, then we would be inclined to say that hitting the man was an accident. If, however, we know that the man was an excellent shot, had a powerful and accurate scope on his rifle, and had recently been having bitter quarrels with the slain man, whom he suspected of having an affair with his wife, then we might suspect murder. In either case, the act is the same. How we understand the act is dependent on how we judge the man's intentions. Likewise in language we have what is said, but how we understand it depends on our judgment of the author's intentions. The words of a statement do not carry meaning—we must go to the heart of the author for this.

3.4 *Illustrations from the Bible*

The difference between what is said and what is meant and, therefore, the necessity of making a judgment about the author's intentions in order to determine the actual sense of words in a passage can be amply illustrated from the Bible. Paul, for example, in 1 Corinthians 12:31 tells the Corinthians to be "jealous" for the most important gifts. Just four verses later, in 13:4, Paul tells them that love, which they are to seek as the highest gift, "is not jealous." Why does Paul tell them first to be jealous, then not to be? Is this just double-talk? The answer is that Paul is using the same Greek word (*zēloūn*) to mean two different things. In the first passages Paul uses it in one sense, and in the second, in another. Indeed, the word is usually translated differently in the two passages. The point is that since there is no rigid relationship between a specific word and a specific meaning, our comprehension of the intentions of Paul is crucial to proper understanding.

In passages where meaning *seems* self-evident, we often forget about the ambiguity of words and the necessity of recognizing the author's intentions. For example, in 1 Corinthians 14:34,35 Paul writes what seems to be a simple, straightforward declaration:

Let the women keep silent in the churches; for they are not permitted to speak, but let them subject themselves, just as the Law also says. And if they desire to learn anything, let them ask their own husbands at home; for it is improper for a woman to speak in church.

What could be more self-evident? Women are to be silent in church. But what does *silent* mean? Not to teach? Sing? Pray? Testify? Make announcements? Preach? All of the above? None of the above? Traditionally, *silent* has often been taken to mean only not to preach— the other vocal activities are allowed. Indeed, in some churches, even the nonvocal activity of voting is considered to be forbidden by this command to be silent. It is clear from the possible options listed above, as well as from the various ones that are actually chosen, that the words *be silent* are ambiguous; that is, a variety of meanings are possible.

In trying to decide on the actual meaning of *silent* however, we must consider Paul and his intentions. What did he mean by the use of this word? In attempting to make such a judgment, several factors must be taken into consideration. Paul, in chapter 11 of this same epistle, has already given instructions for how women are to cover their heads when praying and prophesying in public worship. So it would almost appear that he is contradicting himself here. In fact, since these verses appear at the end of the chapter in some Greek texts, some have argued that these words do not even go back to Paul but are a later insertion. They thus cure the contradiction by "surgery." Another factor is that Paul is perhaps only referring to married women here, for how could unmarried women ask their husbands at home?

When, however, we see that this teaching is set in the general context of Paul's attempt to restore order in public worship by regulating the behavior of Christians in the general *audience* (in previous verses he has spoken about the uses and abuses of tongues, about taking turns, etc.) we perhaps lose the contradiction. He wants to discourage women *in the audience* from talking out of turn, creating and adding to the general confusion in public worship at Corinth—perhaps even at the same time that other women were addressing the congregation according to chapter 11!

An additional consideration in determining Paul's intentions here is his further stipulation that instead of not being silent, they should "ask their husbands at home." Now does such an injunction apply to persons who are speaking or those who are listening? Clearly it is the latter who would have questions of understanding. If then the appeal for women to ask their husbands at home is to correct an abuse to which "be silent" is directed, Paul meant for women in the audience, the listeners, to be silent, not the ones who were addressing the meeting.

This example illustrates well the basic truth about language—there is always a difference between what is said and what is meant. A judgment is inevitable about meaning—the words never speak for themselves. Consequently, any understanding presupposes such an estimate of meaning on our part. The real question is never, Are we going to make such judgments? but rather, Are we going to base our judgments about the meaning of what is written—in this case "to be silent"—on an informed judgment as to the author's intentions when he wrote this, or are we going to use the word as an occasion to sponsor our own understandings (play the Author Game)?

If we do not recognize the distinction between *says* and *means* we will constantly have problems in understanding how authors can write such contradictory things, not only at the level of words and phrases, but also at the level of concepts. For example, if we compare Amos 3:1, 2 with 9:7, we find an apparent contradiction:

Listen Israelites, to these words that the Lord addresses to you, to the whole nation which he brought up from Egypt:

For you alone have I cared among all the nations of the world: Therefore will I punish you for all your iniquities (Amos 3:1, 2, NEB).

Are not you Israelites like the Cushites to me? says the Lord. Did I not bring Israel up from Egypt, the Philistines from Caphtor, the Aramaeans from Kir? (Amos 9:7, NEB.)

The second verse seems clearly at odds with the first. Now several solutions have been suggested. Some claim that 9:7 represents the real Amos, and 3:1,2 is a later addition. Another solution is that in 3:1,2 Amos is reflecting back to the people their own reasoning: They claim that God is with them (5:14) because He has specially chosen them, and they are therefore safe from His judgment. Amos, on the other hand, would draw quite different conclusions. Just because they claim to be specially privileged, they should also expect special retribution for their disobedience. In 3:1,2, then, Amos is challenging the conclusion of the people based on their own premises. Now in 9:7, the situation and intention is different. He seems to be challenging the premise itself. Does Israel really have the special position that it claims to have? Have not other nations experienced God's grace in their history as well? The two statements would then be addressed to different problems with different purposes in mind. To get to the heart of an author's meaning, we must be sensitive to the way he or she is using words. We cannot jump immediately from the words themselves to the meaning of a passage. Instead we arrive at the actual meaning only after we make a judgment about the author's intentions.

3.5 *Intention and the Meaning of Words*

The loose fit between *says* and *means* explains why we can understand the meaning of a passage—an author's intentions—even when the "wrong" words are used. In Isaiah 9:3 we read in the modern translations:

Thou hast increased their joy and given them great gladness (NEB). Actually, the text has literally in the second half of the line, . . . "*not* given great gladness." The King James Version indeed translated it this way. However, it has been recognized since antiquity that the word *not* here was a mistake, that this is not what the author meant to say. Instead, he meant a very similar sounding word translated as "them" above. Even though in this passage the wrong word is written, we can nevertheless understand the meaning. This illustrates for us further the power of the author's intentions in determining meaning.

Likewise in 1 Corinthians 15:5, Paul, relating the tradition about Christ's resurrection, writes, ". . . he appeared to Peter and then to all twelve apostles" (TEV). Judas, of course, was dead by this time. Paul, in using the word *twelve* here, is referring to a body of people known as The Twelve—Jesus' inner circle of disciples—regardless of number. In reading this passage we probably have never even noticed this. Again, we can understand what Paul meant, even if he uses a word, *twelve,* which usually is a counting term for a specific number of objects.

3.6 *Intention and Language Type*

The intentions of an author not only govern the *sense* in which a word is used, but also they determine the *way* in which his language is to be understood. Often we hear people arguing that we ought to take the Bible literally. By this they sometimes mean we ought to understand the Bible in a historical or concrete way, not figuratively. This, of course, is making a judgment about the author's intention in writing. There are many different ways to use language—and biblical authors used a variety of ways to communicate.[3] How is the author of the following story using words, for example?

"Once the trees went forth to anoint a king over them, and they said to the olive tree, 'Reign over us!' But the olive tree said to them, 'Shall I leave my fatness with which God and men are honored, and go to wave over the trees?' Then the trees said to the fig tree, 'You come reign over us!' But the fig tree said to them, 'Shall I leave my sweetness and my good fruit and go to wave over the trees?' Then the trees said to the vine, 'You come, reign over us!' But the vine said to them, 'Shall I leave my new wine, which cheers God and men, and go to wave over the trees?' Finally all the trees said to the bramble, 'You come, reign over us!' And the bramble said to the trees, 'If in truth you are anointing me as king over you, come and take refuge in my shade; but if not, may fire come out from the bramble and consume the cedars of Lebanon'" (Judg. 9:8-15).

It would appear, taking what is written at face value historically, that trees not only talked at one time, but they organized themselves into nations ruled by kings. This, of course, is a preposterous interpretation. Jotham was relating a fable to illustrate to the people of Shechem their folly in making his brother Abimelech king. Nothing could be further from his mind than offering a botanical study. Some might even hold that the figurative understanding of words in a fable is the literal one. In any case, whether we understand the passage as a botanical treatise or as a fable, the words do not change—only the meaning changes. The words are neutral—they can be taken in either way. What *does* make a difference in meaning is our judgment of how the author intended to use words.

3.7 *Conclusion*

The cases above illustrate an important point for us—what is said may have different meanings depending on the intent of the author. To understand someone, consequently, not only involves hearing what they say, but determining what they *mean* by what they say.

The reason we must judge how an author is using his language is that there is only a loose relationship between what is meant and the language used to express this. That is, a specific meaning can be expressed in a variety of ways and likewise specific words may express a variety of thoughts. This difference between form—how something is said, and content—what is said, results in an ambiguity which is basic and inherent to language itself.

Because of this dualism, we must be clear about one fact: All understandings of a text are based on a judgment about the meaning of what is said. There is no "judgmentless" understanding! The real or actual sense of a passage, as the above examples show, grows from our estimate of how it is that the author himself wished the words to be taken. It is clear, then, that *the intention of the author is the one sure standard against which we can measure competing interpretations to ascertain the actual meaning of a passage.*

This shift from literal meaning of a text to the actual meaning as the goal of understanding is more than just a matter of semantics, since it will change the focus of our Bible study and help us to avoid that familiar and tedious disputation as to whether we should take the Bible literally or explain it away through figurative interpretations. Rather the question becomes, What did the author himself intend to communicate? It is no longer a question of whether or not we *can* take a passage in such and such a way, but whether we *should*. Too often arguments about interpretation revolve around either our modern ingenuity in construing things literally or our tolerance for nonsense as a badge of faith. We should not impose our straitjackets on an author, be they literal or figurative ones. The first, most important step in understanding is being considerate of the author's intentions. Remember the golden rule of understanding: Understand another's words as he wants them to be understood, not as we want to understand them. (See 1.7.)

Footnotes
1. See Bibliography, section IV.
2. Beekman and Callow, p. 22.
3. The recognition that the language of the Bible is not "flat"—i.e., of one literary type ("historical")—has opened new horizons in our understanding of Scripture. In a landmark decision for Catholic biblical scholarship, Pope Pius XII wrote:
"The literal sense of a passage is not always as clear in the speech and writing of the ancient authors of the East as it is in the words of writers of our time. What they wished to say cannot be determined simply from the rules of grammar and philology, nor solely from the context. The exegete must go back in spirit to those remote centuries of the East and with the help of history, archaeology, ethnology and other sciences, determine accurately what literary genres the authors of that ancient time could and did use. The ancient peoples of the Orient did not always employ those forms of expression to express their ideas which we use today. Rather they used those familiar to the men of their times and countries. What these were the commentator cannot determine *a priori*, but only after a careful examination of the ancient Oriental literatures." (*Divino afflante Spiritu,* in *Enchiridion biblicum,* nos. 558-60.) Quoted in Dennis J. McCarthy, *Treaty and Covenant* (Rome: Pontifical Biblical Institute, 1963), pp. 10-11.

4 | Aspects of Meaning

4.1 *Meaning and Scope*

In the last chapter we focused on the author's intentions as determining the meaning of a statement. But meaning involves more than just recognizing what content is being communicated. Meaning also involves what effect or function the words were intended to have. If someone says, "Shut the door!" we know that he has certain expectations of us. It is not enough to merely understand his words, but we must also carry out his intentions. The biblical writers, too, wrote with certain expectations in mind. If we are to take them seriously, we must be attentive to how they expected their statements to function.

This aspect of an author's intention is what we call *scope,* that is, what range the author wanted his statement to have. Did he intend his statement to be a generalized principle, or did he intend a specific instruction limited to very definite circumstances? In 1 Timothy 5:23, Paul writes to his friend Timothy, "No longer drink only water, but use a little wine for the sake of your stomach and your frequent ailments" (RSV). This command to stop drinking water has not, of course, been taken very seriously by most Christians. Rather, by placing it in the context of its time, it has been relativized. Since we no longer have a water problem, since we have strong stomachs, and since we have other remedies for our ailments, we need not stop drinking water. Furthermore, since it is addressed to a specific problem of a specific (and perhaps exceptionally ascetic) individual, we need not generalize the command to all Christians today.

With this treatment of 1 Timothy 5:23, we might contrast the usual treatment of 1 Timothy 2:11, 12: "Let a woman quietly receive instruction with entire submissiveness. But I do not allow a woman to teach or exercise authority over a man, but to remain quiet." Often this is taken as Paul's statement characterizing an ideal that is binding on the church. But why do we think that 2:11, 12 is an ideal and to have a general application, while 5:23 is not? Isn't it because 2:11, 12 tends to represent the *status quo* in the church, while 5:23 does not? Should we not rather seek a more objective criterion for deciding on the scope of application than that it agrees with present practice? Instead, we need to ask what scope, what limits of application, the *author* had in mind. Was Paul intending to correct a specific situation with a specific injunction or was he describing the ideal relationship of men and women in the church?

Since we tend to read the Bible so seriously, seeing its statements as loaded with significance, everything the Bible says becomes in our minds a statement of an ideal. The fact is, however, that the statements in the Bible are often criticisms or correctives addressed to particular faults of particular groups of people rather than statements about some abstract ideal. We do a grave injustice to authors when we mistake these criticisms for their ultimate thoughts on the matter. In the prophets, for example, we find a biting criticism of Israelite worship:

"I hate, I reject your festivals, nor do I delight in your solemn assemblies. Even though you offer up to Me burnt offerings and your grain offerings, I will not accept them; and I will not even look at the peace offerings of your fatlings. Take away from Me the noise of your songs. I will not even listen to the sound of your harps. But let justice roll down like waters and righteousness like an ever-flowing stream" (Amos 5:21-24).

Since we do not regularly worship God in this way, it is easy for us to assume that this is a blanket indictment of the whole sacrificial system. But in fact, this is not so much an indictment of this form of worship as it is an indictment of the worshipers. What Amos goes on, in the passage, to call for is "justice and righteousness," not some form of formal worship that ought to be practiced.

This accounts for the fact that a prophet can attack the people's worship, but see the same form of worship being practiced in the future. Jeremiah is a good example of this:

"For what purpose does frankincense come to Me from Sheba, and the sweet cane from a distant land? Your burnt offerings are not acceptable, and your sacrifices are not pleasing to Me" (6:20).

But later in the book in 33:18 we find:

"And the Levitical priests shall never lack a man before Me to offer burnt offerings, to burn grain offerings, and to prepare sacrifices continually."

We must not mistake statements of criticism for statements of principle. As we study Scripture, we must decide inductively in each case what scope the passage was intended to have.

4.2 *Meaning and Significance*

Much of the confusion about understanding language, especially language in the Bible, arises because we do not distinguish carefully enough between two different kinds of meaning that language has. The word *meaning* in English is used, on the one hand, for what the author of a passage intends to communicate. We also use *meaning* for what it is that a reader understands or comprehends. We say, "I found this passage very meaningful," or "It didn't mean a thing to me." In English, then, we use the word *meaning* for both the author's meaning and the reader's meaning.

Now since we usually do not specify which meaning we are talking about, we might easily confuse them and the respective roles to which they refer—who is the audience and who is the author. It will be helpful in order to clarify our thinking to use two different words for these two concepts. *Meaning* we shall reserve for what the author intends his words to mean. *Significance* is their meaningfulness, the meaning they have for the reader. [1]

To illustrate, let us take a rather homely example. When a parent addresses a command to a child, such as "Shut the door," the parent expects two things to happen—the child shall understand what is being said (both content and scope) and do what is asked. The child is to realize the significance of the command and to make the appropriate application. Now if the child does not respond appropriately—and shuts the window instead—the parent may repeat the statement, assuming the child did not understand what was said. If, however, the child ignores the command, the parent may reprimand him, not because the child did not understand—but exactly because he *did* understand but did not obey. The child, on the other hand, might explain that he ignored the command because it didn't make sense, from his perspective, to do it. Let us say the house was hot and he had just opened the door in order to cool it, or that the parent was coming up the walk with large bags of groceries, or a variety of other reasons. Given such an explanation for his lack of application, the parent would realize why the child regarded the command as having little significance in his present situation.

We can see from this example that we can and do differentiate constantly between the recognition of others' meaning when they speak or write to us and our own individual response to it based on our own thinking in our situation. The two processes, although related, are distinct—our understanding of another person and our own estimate of its application, importance, and meaningfulness to us.

The author should determine the meaning of his words. The readers, on the other hand, determine the significance—the meaning that the passage holds for them and for others. The following diagram may help illustrate this:

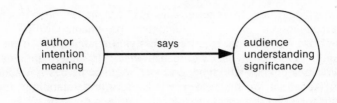

It is important to keep this distinction in mind between meaning and significance, since one of the most frequent errors in Bible study comes from confusing them. People often, or perhaps even usually, read the Bible for some insight or thought which is meaningful to them. When they discover a meaningful interpretation, they accept it as valid understanding of the text, since the truth of the interpretation is guaranteed by the meaning it has for them personally. On the contrary, we must recognize that just because a person has found a meaningful interpretation, does not mean that it is the correct one—that is, one related to what the author wanted to say. (See chapter 1.) To thus confuse significance (meaning for the reader) with meaning (what the author intended) is to make the reader the author rather than the audience. Our first task, then, in reading, is to find out what the *author* is saying.

This distinction between meaning and significance helps us understand why it sometimes seems as if the meaning of the Bible changes. It would, of course, be more correct to say that our understanding of it changes and with this, its significance for us. But even if our understanding did not change, the significance would still do so, since this is tied to our circumstances within which we are making application. What sometimes unfortunately happens is that mistaking the significance for the meaning, we feel that to change our application is somehow to change the meaning of Scripture. It does not change its meaning, but rather its meaning for us. It is actually our circumstances that have changed.

The history of the church's understanding and application of the Bible can be visualized as a constant with two variables. The constant is the author's meaning, which we discussed in the previous chapter. The two variables are the church's own comprehension of this meaning and its application of it. The following diagram illustrates this:

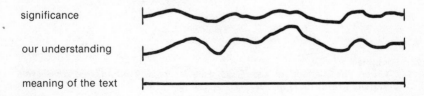

What is important to recognize is that no matter how much our understanding or application fluctuates, the meaning which spawns these does not change. It is this underlying meaning which we keep seeking. Since, however, we realize that our understandings and applications change with time, we must not become overly wedded to them. Above all, we must never mistake our understandings and the significance that this has for us, for the author's meaning.

4.3 *Summary*

I have tried to illustrate in this part that when our goal is to understand the Bible, we need to carefully uncover the actual meaning of a passage, that is, how the author intended it to be understood. Adopting this as our goal, we can avoid the usually futile "literal" versus "figurative" argument, since we don't assume either as the basis for our interpretation; but by working inductively, we uncover clues in the text that help us decide how a statement was meant to be understood. In this way we are in a position to listen to an author and to receive from him, rather than to give his words our own meanings. Our best means of avoiding the pitfall of attributing our meanings to another's words is the recognition that there is no immediate understanding in language, but all is mediated through our judgments as to meaning. Being aware of this mediation, we can try to build a solid factual basis for our judgments. We have also seen that this actual meaning has at least two major aspects—the content which is being communicated and its intended function, or scope. On the other hand, the meaning that a passage has for us we termed the *significance* of the passage. While the actual meaning of a passage is set by the author and remains constant through time, the significance this has for others may change as their understanding and circumstances change.

Footnotes
1. For this distinction, see E. D. Hirsch, *Validity in Interpretation* (Yale University Press, 1967), p. 33.

PART III | # How Understanding Works

"It takes a great listener to hear what is actually said, a greater one to hear what was not said, but comes to light in the speaking."

Palmer, Hermeneutics

"Thus a person who seeks to understand must question what lies behind what is said. He must understand it as an answer to a question. If we go back behind what is said, then we inevitably ask questions beyond what is said."

Gadamer, Truth and Method

5 | The Tacit Dimension and Understanding

5.1 *The Tacit Dimension*

As we have seen in the last section, words by themselves can have a variety of legitimate meanings. It is only when used by an author in context that they can be assigned a specific meaning. If we stop to think a moment, it will be evident that we assign words a specific meaning based not on what is said, but on what is *meant* in the saying. Before entering church on Sunday morning, we may strictly charge our children to be quiet in church. But if that morning the minister has a lesson for the children, and he asks our Johnny, "Who killed Goliath?" we will be rather surprised if Johnny keeps quiet. We may ask him afterward, "Why didn't you answer the minister? You know very well that David killed Goliath!" If Johnny replies, "But you told us to be quiet in church!" we may be a bit exasperated. "That may be what I said, but you didn't understand what I meant when I said that."

When we speak, we assume a tacit dimension—a host of assumptions about language which form the basis of our communication. These assumptions are of two kinds: the normal customary conventions that operate within language, and the external context within which we speak. Likewise, it is on the basis of these unspoken assumptions that we understand what is said. Learning what these assumptions are is a necessary part of learning to use and understand the words of a language. This is why children make mistakes about meaning. They have not yet grasped this tacit dimension. In this respect, language is like an iceberg. Most of it is not visible, but the part that is invisible is nevertheless as important as the visible. We neglect the tacit dimension only at the risk of shipwreck.

This explains why so-called literal interpretations often resemble the common misunderstandings of children. Neither has a good grasp of the tacit dimension—the assumptions needed for proper understanding.

5.2 *The Tacit Dimension Within Language*

Whenever language is sensibly written or spoken it contains features which help us make correct judgments as to meaning. Some of these factors can be observed from what is said. For example, Paul writes in Romans 14:2, ". . . a weaker man eats only vegetables" (RSV). Now Paul does not mean here that the *physically* weak should be vegetarians, but rather *those weaker in the faith.* We know this because in the first verse of the chapter Paul writes, "If a man is weak in his faith. . ." Thus implicit in Paul's use of the word *weak* in the second verse is the definition of the term that he has already given in verse 1. The tacit dimension in language is that part which, though unspoken or unexpressed, is assumed to be understood.

Another feature of the implicit part of language is that we speak according to rules or conventions. By this is meant not grammar and proper usage, but unwritten rules such as, "If you command someone to do something, you assume that the person is able to perform the action." For example, when the March Hare told Alice to have some wine (see the quotation at the beginning of Part II) she was understandably surprised, since there was only tea at the table. We sometimes forget how important these conventions are to our use and understanding of language because they are so automatic that they are a reflex with us. But they are essential to understanding and usage.

Thus in order to understand someone, we must know the type of language being used and the rules this type of language presupposes. For example, in Amos 9:7 we have a question, usually translated, "'Are you not like the Ethiopians to me, O people of Israel?' says the Lord" (RSV). The type of question found here can, however, represent a usage in Hebrew in which the speaker makes a strong positive assertion whose truth is unconditionally admitted. We should, then, translate with the *Good News Bible*: "The Lord says, 'People of Israel, I think as much of the people of Sudan as I do of you.' " Amos is not asking the people a question. He is telling them something they should regard as quite certain. Knowing about this convention affects the way we understand the words of Amos in this passage.

Another related feature of the implicit dimension of language is that the conventions of a language not only specify what conditions are presupposed, but also what domain or range the words are to have. (See 4.1.) Limiting circumstances, ramifications, and possible contingencies are seldom spelled out. For example, in a library we might see a sign which proclaims boldly in large block letters, SILENCE! This sign means that in the ordinary course of business in the library, one is not to make so much noise as to disturb others. It does not mean that in case of emergency one should not yell, *"Fire!"* Although not stated, it is tacitly presupposed that in such circumstances the rule no longer applies. All language depends on people making such commonsense, practical judgments about the range of application.

Parents often run afoul of their children because, as we have suggested, children have not yet learned these facts about language. When a child asks, "Dad, will you play ball with me after supper?" his father may say yes. But after supper something comes up so that the father cannot play ball. The father, if accused by the son of lying, will stoutly deny this. "When I said I would play ball with you after supper, I meant. . . ," and he will proceed to unload some implicit features of this statement. The boy, a bit sadder but wiser, when he next asks his father to play, may say, "Dad, will you *promise* to play ball with me after supper?" To promise something as opposed to just "saying" something has certain implicit conventions and rules, which the son now wishes to impose on his father. The father may be reluctant to promise—to be bound by the implicit conventions of promising. In short, *to know the implicit conventions of a language is crucial to understanding what is meant by what is said.*

5.3 *The Tacit Dimension Outside of Language*

We have labeled this feature the *tacit* dimension instead of the *implicit* dimension because not all the factors we use in making judgments about the meaning of language are implicit in language. Some of these factors belong to the nonlinguistic environment, the *context* within which language is being used. If a child, for example, suddenly shouts, "I see the white house," it makes a difference whether the family is on tour in Washington, D.C., or is following directions to find a friend's house, and a crucial part of the directions was to turn left after passing the white house on the south side of the road. The meaning of these two statements is different because they tacitly presuppose different circumstances and assumptions on the part of both the hearer and the speaker. Or again, if someone says, "Will you please pick up my mail this morning and bring it here?" it may be the polite request of a friend asking a favor of another friend. But if a boss says this to the secretary, it is not a request, but a (polite) command. The external tacit dimension is here crucial to the conventions that apply and how the request is understood.

It is also from context that we can distinguish which sense of an ambiguous statement is meant. The sentence "Tuesday's arrival was eagerly anticipated" in the context of a family awaiting the arrival of a daughter named Tuesday means one thing. In the context of a school class who are going on an exciting field trip on Tuesday, the meaning is something else. This illustrates the tremendous importance of context for meaning. If you change the setting of a statement, you may change its meaning. Thus the background against which you see a statement will exert a major influence on how you understand it. *To understand the actual sense of Scripture, we must see Scripture in its own authentic, historical context.*

In Mark 2:15-17 the Pharisees are complaining because Jesus eats with tax collectors and sinners. We have found that when we study this passage with people, they almost invariably assume that the problem here is Jesus' *associating* with sinners. The passage, of course, plainly says the Pharisees were troubled because Jesus *ate* with sinners. In our context, eating has no special connotation. In Jesus' day, however, as among Jews today, the way food is prepared, what food is eaten, and what foods are eaten together are of great importance. Jesus was evidently violating the religious food laws of His day by taking His meal with sinners.

5.4 *Practical Inferences*

But how do we make use of the tacit dimension to arrive at meaning? How do we know what tacit dimension a speaker or writer is presupposing when he or she uses language? Since the mind of the speaker—even less a writer of long ago—is not open to direct inspection, we make judgments about the tacit dimension on the basis of what we might call *practical inferences*—that is, how a rational or normal author of these words would reasonably expect them to be understood.

The problem is that often several normal or rational explanations may be possible. As a teacher, I have observed that true-false questions tend to penalize the brighter students. In reading through a question they are often able to supply one set of inferences which would make the meaning of the statement false, and another that would make it true. It is then a matter of guessing which set of inferences the instructor had in mind. How do we decide which set of inferences is the right one? Is it only a matter of opinion—just a shot in the dark?

We each do, indeed, have our own ideas as to what is the normal or rational meaning of a statement. This is true because we have our own opinions or presuppositions about what words mean and imply and how they should be used. These presuppositions are, in fact, necessary; they enable us to choose the right words to express ourselves when we speak or write. Just as they guide us in our own communication, they also guide us in understanding others. Our understanding, then, is necessarily based on these subjective opinions. From this one might argue that there can obviously be no objective understanding or interpretation. All interpretation must be to some extent biased—that is, reflect our own presuppositions. Therefore, we can never determine what is the one correct understanding of a text.

This type of argument would seem to undermine a major premise of the second section—that meaning can be determined and that we need to sort out the correct interpretation from the incorrect ones. If we reflect a bit about our everyday experiences with language, however, we realize that we can and do understand specific meanings intended by other people, even with our subjective presuppositions. We even know that at times we misunderstand—make incorrect judgments about the meaning of statements. Likewise we know that others understand us, as well as misunderstand us. From our own experience, in short, we believe we are capable of telling incorrect understandings from correct ones. To use language, then, implies that a correct, determinate, ascertainable meaning can be expressed and understood. To deny this is to deny both the nature and function of language.

But why is this so? How is it possible that we do, in fact, understand and make correct judgments about what others say constantly in daily life? First, we share a good many unspoken conventions and assumptions with other language users. For example, we assume a relationship between the customary use of words—their normal meaning—and people's intent when they are used. This happens even though people do not always use words correctly. For instance, for some people the word *well* is an adverb and qualifies verbs—it tells how well something was done; while *good,* on the other hand, is an adjective and qualifies nouns—it tells how good something is. For other people, however, the word *good* serves both functions. For those who make the distinction, the sentence "You did good" means that you did a good thing, as opposed to "You did well," which means that you did an action, such as reading or running, proficiently. Those who do not make the distinction would say, "You did good," to express both meanings. Now, although there is clearly a difference in usage and assumed conventions as to what is considered the normal or the correct meaning of the word *good,* both those who do and those who do not make the distinction between *good* and *well,* understand each other. Differences in presuppositions do not make understanding impossible. It is not just a matter of opinion or a guess as to what a speaker means when he says, "You did good." Of course, the more of these conventions—the greater the tacit dimension held in common—the easier understanding becomes.

Since all language usage and understanding is based on these assumed conventions (the tacit dimension), the correct interpretation does not depend on reaching the impossible goal of a completely objective interpretation (one that is based on no presuppositions at all), but rather on an understanding based on the presuppositions of the author. We must find a way to get into the world of an author—the tacit dimension of his statements. *The practical inferences which lead to a correct understanding—a determination of the actual meaning of another's words—are those which are based on the tacit dimension which undergirds the author's language.*

This leads to the second element which makes understanding possible: We can, in fact, enter into another's tacit dimension. We can transcend our own presuppositions and recognize those of another, even those which we do not share. We have, in short, the capacity for empathy. We understand the behavior of others even though we would not act as they do, because we have insight into why they act as they do. We use this capacity frequently when we try to anticipate how people will respond to our own actions or statements. We say to ourselves, "From what I know of so and so, he or she will think. . ." This empathy which leads to understanding another is not some mystical emotion, not a type of private intuition, but rather is developed from clues which are open to inductive analysis.

Anthropological literature is full of cases of misunderstanding due to *lack* of observation and induction. Instead, interpretations were based on the observer's own idea of what a custom or action meant. This type of deductive process applied to the behavior or actions of others is called *ethnocentrism.* It is the habit of deciding the meaning of something on the basis of one's *own* context and thought rather than that of the actor or the speakers. In biblical study as well, we need to safeguard the text from our ethnocentrism, using our own presuppositions to explain it. This is the opposite of empathy and understanding.

In the example given above of Amos's question in 9:7 ("Are you not like the Ethiopians to me?"), as long as we understand this text on the basis of our conventions in the English language regarding questions, we will try to force his words into an alien mold. We will judge by our own standards. When, however, we understand the conventions of Hebrew regarding questions, we will begin to empathize, and our understanding of Amos will be based on inferences grounded in his tacit dimension, not ours.

5.5 *Conclusion*

Because of the difference between what is said and what is meant, we must rely on the tacit dimension to determine what is meant. The tacit dimension has two aspects; that found within language itself and that part dependent on external circumstances. Within language we must consider relationships between sentences, paragraphs, and the type of language used and its conventions. Externally we must examine the circumstances of writing which are relevant for understanding.

We make use of the tacit dimension through making practical inferences about the author's intention. Empathy—the ability to see things from another point of view—plays a major part in this. Without this empathy we will be ethnocentric, interpreting things according to our own point of view instead of the author's. Using our diagram to illustrate this concept, we would picture it thus:

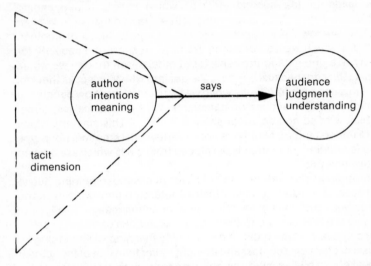

What is said depends on the tacit dimension behind it for its meaning.

6 | Induction and Understanding

6.1 *Induction and Deduction*

As we have seen, to comprehend another's intention may be the first step to correct understanding, but how can we be sure that we are in fact comprehending, rather than seeing what we want to see in the text? The major safeguard we have for preserving the author's intentions is to operate as inductively as possible, rather than deductively.

By induction we mean beginning with observations rooted in the text itself from which interpretations are constructed. To operate deductively, on the other hand, is to believe or hold some rule or principle in advance and then to explain the text in terms of this belief. In induction we base our understanding of a text on the clues (data) found in the text and its tacit dimension—clues which can be shown to any other reader for consideration. Deduction, however, brings to the text certain ideas about its meaning. These ideas are usually statements of belief to which one needs to give assent in advance of looking at the text, since they are not rooted in the text itself.

Several years ago, I gave a guest lecture in a conservative seminary. All during the lecture, the students kept looking to the teacher to see if what I said was correct. They needed to know if what I said agreed with or infringed upon the statement of faith which the seminary held concerning the Bible. The teacher would occasionally indicate to them that what I was saying was all right, that it didn't undermine their doctrinal position. The students were not free to examine what I said on its own merits and to accept or reject it on the basis of the evidence. Instead, they (or their teachers) had determined ahead of time what was acceptable—what the Bible could say.

Strictly speaking, no interpretation is either purely inductive or deductive, but each must be kept in its place. The general rule is that induction must precede deduction; that is, we must get the facts *before* we draw our conclusions so that deduction does not influence the process of induction. We must not exclude some clues simply because they do not agree with either the conclusions we want to draw or what we now believe. If we seriously wish to let the biblical writers speak for themselves, we must understand on the basis of what can be known about the text itself, rather than what is believed about the text.

We must realize that we all come to the Bible with a good deal of "baggage"—assumptions about the text—since we have long accepted traditions about how we are to understand the Bible. In fact, we often unconsciously supply the author's intentions deductively from our interpretive tradition. For example, the Book of Jonah is taken by many as a historical narrative. After all, it says right in the text that all this happened, with no disclaimers to the contrary! (But we remember that Jotham, in our earlier example, did not think it necessary to tell his audience that he was relating a fable rather than actual fact.) When we look at the text itself, it would appear that there are things in the Book of Jonah that are not literally true—that it was a three days' walk through Nineveh or that there were in Nineveh 120,000 men who did not know right from left.[1] In spite of this, what makes the historical understanding of this story seem right to us instinctively is that this is how we have been taught—it is our interpretive tradition which supplies this authorial intent for us, not clues which we have found in the book itself.

Now let us be clear about what is at stake here. It is not that something strange is reported, for those who hold that a large fish swallowed Jonah would not argue on the basis of Jotham's fable that God made trees talk. Nor is it a question of belief in God's power—to say that God *can* do everything is not to say that He *did* do everything. To say that either Jotham's fable or the Jonah story is possible with God is not to say that either or both actually happened. The real question is not how much we *can* believe, but what we *ought* to believe—How did the author intend the story to be taken: as a historical narrative or as a parabolic story? To answer this we need concrete information about the author and his story from which we can make an inference about his intentions. This issue cannot be decided ahead of time deductively if we want to get a true understanding.

If we would reflect for a moment on how we commonly understand Scripture, we can see that there is nothing unusual in making a judgment about a story as historical or figurative, based upon our notion of reality. For example, in the narrative of Gideon (Judges 6-8) we have the episode of the fleece (Judges 6:36-40) where Gideon gets a sign from God. A little later in the story, in describing Gideon's opponents, the text says, "Their camels were without number, as the sand which is upon the seashore." Now if this were true, there would not have been enough room in all Israel for this many camels. Obviously this description is not to be taken literally. Now the question is, On what basis do we decide about the fleece—that the description there, although it does not correspond to reality, is to be taken as factual—while in the case of the camels, we decide that it is not?

The point of the illustration is not to determine how we make a decision, but simply to underline the fact that as we read Scripture, we are constantly making practical inferences—judgments—about how we understand things. The question can never be, Do we always take things literally or factually? but, On what *basis* do we make such judgments? Since everyone is necessarily making such judgments, the major question is, Do we make these judgments on the basis or our own ideas, beliefs, and feelings, or do we seek a basis in the text, the author, and his world? It is in doing the latter that we end our gamesmanship and begin objective, inductive Bible study.

Another kind of "baggage" which we sometimes bring to the text is our own modern understanding of particular concepts. We then deductively find our meaning in the Bible rather than inductively discovering the writer's meaning. For example, let us examine Hal Lindsay's interpretation of Deuteronomy 18:22:

When a prophet speaks in the name of the Lord, if the word does not come to pass or come true, that is a word which the Lord has not spoken (RSV).

From this verse Lindsay concluded that the sign of a true prophet was his predictive ability, his accuracy in foretelling the future. "Anything less [than 100 percent accuracy of prediction] would doom the prophet to death by stoning," writes Lindsay, using Deuteronomy 13:1-5 as evidence.[2] The curious thing is that the prophet who is about to be stoned in 13:1 is the one who has predicted something with 100 percent accuracy! What apparently happened is that Lindsay brought to the text his own assumption that a true prophet predicts things that happen, while a false prophet predicts things that do not. That this is not the Bible's teaching is overlooked because of his assumption.

If we look at Deuteronomy 18:22 again carefully, we can see that it treats the case of false prediction as only one sign of false prophecy, and it does not necessarily suggest that the opposite (true prediction equals true prophecy) is true. In addition, if we study the careers of true prophets in the Old Testament, we will find that there were cases in which their predictions did not come true.

For example, the prophets Micah and Isaiah were active roughly at the same time in the Southern Kingdom of Judah. Micah predicted the fall of Jerusalem (Mic. 3:12) but Isaiah predicted the opposite (Is. 34:35). Both were taken as true prophets of God, not because they could predict the future, but because they had a message from God for their time. It was, in fact, precisely because Micah's contemporaries took his message seriously that the Lord changed His mind and the prediction did not come true (Jer. 26:16-19). We will therefore need to reject both the modern idea that a true prophet is one who predicts things that come true and all attempts to deductively force the Bible to fit this ideal. Instead, we should inductively search for a truly biblical definition.

It is important to guard against supplying our own intentions or definitions deductively in place of the author's in order to twist them to our own ends, even if it appears that we are allowing them to simply speak for themselves. *In our study of the biblical text, induction must precede deduction.*

6.2 *Clues and Reasons*

We saw in the last chapter that our practical inferences about the meaning of language need to be rational. This means, as we have just seen, that they must be grounded in an inductive process which uses clues found in the text and in the author's situation. This process of estimating an author's meaning, however, really involves us in two types of processes. First, there is the discovery, use, and evaluation of the clues which we use as the basis for our practical inferences. We should be able to list these or show them to anyone who wants to know how we arrived at our interpretation. Secondly, there are the reasons or "warrants" we use which allow us to infer our conclusions from the facts or clues. *The adequacy of our practical inferences must be judged by the clues on which they are based and how well our warrants account for this data.*

Let us say, for example, that we claim that the Romans executed Jesus because they considered Him a political threat. This is our conclusion or interpretation of the event. How can we support this? We might say that the Romans chose to execute Him by crucifixion (the clue or data). But what allows us to go from this clue to our conclusion? We might claim as our "warrant" that the Romans used crucifixion for political enemies. Therefore, we infer that they considered Jesus a political enemy. Now that we have shown our data and what warrants our conclusion, our interpretation can be intelligently disputed. Since few would question the data involved, the "warrant" might be the focus of dispute. Perhaps the Romans used crucifixion for other types of criminals as well (the thieves on the cross, for example). If it were shown that they often did, this would certainly affect the strength of our reasoning and, consequently, the probability of our explanation. [3]

All too often, however, in our discussion of Scriptures we become bogged down in the discussion of our *opinions* about the meaning of a text. No wonder that often our Bible "study" becomes stilted—leading either to a heated debate about unshakable beliefs (or should we say prejudices) or to a polite nodding of heads as each shares an opinion about the text. Rather, we should be searching for and exchanging clues. We should be articulating what reasons or "warrants" exist for drawing the inferences we draw from the data. This would be both exciting and informative.

6.3 *Summary*

Because of the natural ambiguity of language, the tacit dimension becomes critical for our understanding of language. This means that in our study of the Bible we must devote our time to the discovery of clues from which we can reconstruct this dimension. This may seem a fairly abstract approach to understanding language, but we are constantly doing this whenever we are reading or listening to others. Likewise, since in our study of the Bible this tacit dimension is necessary to understanding, *it is not a question of whether or not we will make such practical inferences based on a tacit dimension, but which tacit dimension will we use—the author's or our own.* If we would hear the author, we must understand his statements in his context, not ours.

Illustrating this graphically with our diagram we have the following:

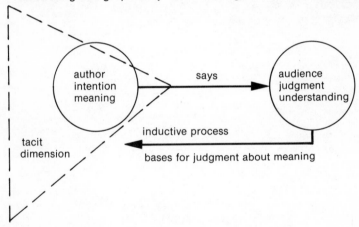

Seeing the author and what is said in the perspective of his tacit dimension brings about real understanding.

Footnotes

1. The tortuous path that so-called literal interpretation must take at times is nicely illustrated by an example from Keil and Delitzch's commentary on Jonah 4:11b. The phrase is literally translated "Men who do not know between their right and their left." Keil and Delitzsch are not able to accept this literal meaning. Instead, they want to read "children" instead of "men." The Hebrew word here is ʾadam, usually translated "man," "men," or "mankind." Keil and Delitzsch give no

evidence of any occurrence where it means "children." Indeed, Hebrew has other words to say "children"—*yeled, ben,* etc. Likewise with *right* and *left.* They do not want to take this literally, but rather figuratively in the sense of "lacking moral knowledge." (Since even children know right from left!) Again, no evidence is given that this is a legitimate meaning of the Hebrew expression. In fact, we would have expected something like "good and evil" if this is what the author intended. (See Deut. 1:39, ". . . your children [*benim*] who do not yet know good and evil. . ." [NEB].) This would be what we should find in Jonah 4:11*b* if Keil and Delitzsch's understanding were correct. In order to take the story literally, they are forced to violate the words of the story—to take them figuratively so that they can be taken literally. (This example was brought to my attention by Wayne Leamans, though for a different purpose.) Carl F. Keil and Franz Delitzsch, *Old Testament Commentaries* (Grand Rapids: Eerdmans).

2. Hall Lindsay, *The Late Great Planet Earth* (Kentwood, Mich.: Zondervan, 1976), p. 10.

3. For further discussion of this example and the point at issue, see Van A. Harvey, *The Historian and the Believer* (New York: Macmillan, 1969), pp. 49-59.

PART IV | Understanding as Perspective

A microphone swung toward him, and the world heard that first strange nonword of his reign.

"... uuuuv?"

The voice was unnatural, pitched above its normal tone.

Holding out his arms, he seemed to be choking. He said the nonword again.

"... uuuuv?"

The people picked up the nonword and made a chant of it, and a new roar began.

On the tapes later, some people thought the word was love.

Others said that the word was a mystic code known only to a few others about the world.

No one heard the question mark.

Thomas Klise, The Last Western

7 | The Compositional Perspective

7.1 *Types of Clues*

In the last chapter we have argued that if we are to understand another, it is best to proceed inductively, using clues to uncover the tacit dimension of a statement, and from this to draw conclusions as to its meaning. When we understand a statement, we can say we are seeing it in perspective—in the context necessary for its correct understanding. But what are these clues which help us do this? What are we looking for?

The clues are of three types. Some we find in the composition itself, some are found in the situation in which it was written and to which it was directed, and some involve motivation—that is, why the statement was made. In the following three chapters, we will illustrate how these clues enable us to understand. Because of lack of space we will not give extended analyses of any of the passages. We intend only to point to the paths to be taken, not to provide a road map. Hopefully the brevity will not obscure the point being illustrated.

7.2 *Composition*

The immediate literary context in which something is said or written is crucial to understanding a statement. Even in statements that appear to be simple declarations, a "literal" understanding can sometimes cause problems if their context is not considered. For example, in Matthew 5:39, Jesus declares, ". . . But whoever slaps you on your right cheek, turn to him the other also." Taking this literally, I reason that Jesus is talking about the right cheek, so if someone strikes me on the left, I can still obey Jesus and not turn my other cheek. Here, of course, such a plain literal sense leads one astray. In this case, the context clearly guards against such a mistake, since this specific command is preceded by the more general statement, "But I say to you, do not resist him who is evil." Jesus then gives being slapped on the right cheek and turning the other as a specific example of this general principle, which would also include being slapped on the left cheek. Thus, while it would literally be true that Jesus says to turn the other cheek only when one is slapped on the right, it would clearly be a mistaken understanding of this command in its present context to interpret it as a legal statement rather than as an illustration.

Another way in which a composition gives clues to a passage's meaning is in its structure. Looking at the arrangement of contents, seeing the structure of a work is often invaluable for understanding it. Discovering the structure of Deuteronomy, for example, can revolutionize our understanding of its message. In rough outline, Deuteronomy begins with a short section giving the setting of the words and identifying the speaker. Next come several chapters in which Israel's recent history is recounted. This in turn is followed by a legal section in chapters 5—26. In chapters 5—11, the style is sermonic, with many exhortations to obedience. In chapter 12 and following, the laws are much more specific. From chapter 27 on, there is a variety of material—instructions for a covenant renewal ceremony, blessings and curses which follow either obedience or disobedience, and the giving over of the scroll to the Levites for safekeeping. This structure seems to follow in loose outline the structure that can be found elsewhere in Old Testament times in political treaties made between an emperor and a vassal prince. This has led to the conclusion that Deuteronomy is a treaty document—a treaty between God as king and the people as His vassals. Once this is seen, then we can in part understand the language in Deuteronomy as political language. This in turn illuminates our understanding of individual passages in Deuteronomy. For example, in Deuteronomy 6:4, 5, the greatest commandment, the command to "love the Lord," can now be understood today as a command to pledge allegiance to God. From understanding the structure of a composition, we gain a perspective on how to understand the words.

7.3 *The Type of Writing*

The way in which something is written, the type of literature which an author writes, is also an important clue for our understanding. When we hear a statement today, its manner is inferred from the tone of voice, the appearance of the speaker, and the inflection pattern—question, command, etc. In reading, however, we often do not have this type of clue to guide us. Instead, we draw our conclusions from the way in which something is written. If a narrative begins, "Once upon a time. . . ," we expect a type of fiction; while a story which begins, "On July 14, 1932. . ." leads us to expect history. Likewise, when Jesus begins a story with the phrase "The kingdom of heaven is like...," we infer that He is presenting a parable, a figurative story to illustrate a point, rather than an actual occurrence. Or again, when a narrative begins, "In the beginning...," we can reasonably assume that we are not dealing with history in the usual sense of the term, but with something suprahistorical—before history. These assumptions about the manner or type of writing are crucial to our further understanding of the content.

Different types of language are used for different kinds of truths. Language is often used to convey more than just factual, narrative content. For example, in 2 Samuel 12:1-4, Nathan the prophet relates the following story to David:

> "There were two men in one city, the one rich and the other poor. The rich man had a great many flocks and herds. But the poor man had nothing except one little ewe lamb which he bought and nourished; and it grew up together with him and his children. It would eat of his bread and drink of his cup and lie in his bosom, and was like a daughter to him. Now a traveler came to the rich man. And he was unwilling to take from his own flock or his own herd, to prepare for the wayfarer who had come to him; rather he took the poor man's ewe lamb and prepared it for the man who had come to him."

David's immediate reply was that the culprit was as good as dead. Nathan then turned the tables on David and said, "You are the man!" for David had acted similarly in taking Bathsheba for his wife. David, of course, had been "set up" by Nathan's story. It was not an actual legal case which called for the king's decision, but rather a story with another purpose—to make clear to him the truth about his own behavior. David did not reply to Nathan's accusation, "Oh, the story is a fiction, eh? Well, I guess that lets me off the hook!" Instead, he got the point and repented of his wrongdoing. The fact that the story is not historically true does not mean that it isn't true. Conversely, to demand that all language be understood in the same way as "historically true" is to miss the point many times. If God's truth is so limited that it can only be related through factual narratives, then why did Jesus teach in parables?

Sometimes, however, we need not only to infer the type of language used, but even the inflectional pattern used. In Luke 22:36-38, Jesus is telling His disciples of the difficulties that lie ahead. When the disciples reply that they have "two swords," Jesus says, "It is enough." Now a straightforward statement about the sufficiency of two swords for the defense of Jesus and His disciples would be one possible interpretation. But in this context, with the disciples—as is so often the case in the Gospels—not quite understanding the situation, and keeping in mind Jesus' later rebuke of Peter for his use of the sword, we might also reasonably infer that Jesus used either a tone of irony or one of resignation, expressing His frustration with their slowness to catch on.

7.4 *Content Comparison*

Besides looking at the structure, the immediate context in the composition, and the type of writing, we also need to compare the topic or theme of a particular passage with other occurrences of the theme in the book. For example, in 1 Corinthians, chapter 8 is devoted to eating food offered to idols. Here Paul invokes the principle of love for one's fellow as a guide. This principle is contrasted with knowledge— knowledge which is unconcerned with human consequences. These themes of food, knowledge, and love are also found in 1 Corinthians 6:12-20 and 10:14-22, with a related passage in 9:19-23. (Note how this latter illustrates 10:31—11:1.) An adequate understanding of chapter 8 will be gained only when it is seen in the perspective of these other similar passages.

In the study of the prophets it is hard to know how to get a foothold. Often we end up choosing a "motto" verse and letting this stand as the message of the prophet. A more profitable way to proceed is to take, for example, all the accusations which the prophet brings against the people. In comparing and classifying them, the major concerns of the prophet will become evident. In addition we will gain some perspective on how the individual accusations fit into the whole of the message.

7.5 *Conclusion*

To begin seeing a passage in correct perspective, we begin with an analysis of the composition to which it belongs and the type of language in which it is written.

8 | The Historical Perspective

8.1 *Situation*

The situation within which something is said or written is often the single most important factor in understanding. (See 5.3.) It can even compensate for the misuse of language itself. For example, if we are in a hot room with the door open and the windows closed and someone says, "Let's open some doors and get some fresh air," we would probably begin opening the windows. We knew what was meant from context, even though it wasn't said. For the biblical material, we can consider at least three major contexts which aid our understanding—the specific context, the general context, and the linguistic context.

8.2 *Specific Context*

The specific context is the immediate context of a statement—the specific situation in which or to which it was written, and its place within the author's thought. In many of Paul's letters, for example, he is writing about specific problems in congregations—often problems caused by the newness of the church and of their Christian faith. In Corinthians, especially, this is true. Paul is writing to correct specific situations and answering questions about which they have requested guidance. One can see clues which point to this in phrases such as "It is actually reported that. . ." and "Now concerning the things about which you wrote. . . ." In interpreting such passages we need to see them as correctives of disturbed situations, not as ideal principles.

The general theological perspective of an author must also be considered as part of the specific context of a statement. This is because in understanding the more specific statements of an author, we must see them in the perspective of the general principles or premises which guided him. This is especially true in the cases just mentioned in Paul's letters where his specific advice must be related to his general principles. For example, in understanding Paul's statement, "Let the women keep silent in the churches. . ." (1 Cor. 14:33-36) it is important to see this not only as a corrective, but to remember Paul's more general principle of equality for all in Christ:

> There is neither Jew nor Greek, there is neither slave nor free man, there is neither male nor female; for you are all one in Christ Jesus (Gal. 3:28).

Furthermore, elsewhere Paul sets forth as a general principle that Christians should not offend others in the exercise of their Christian freedom (1 Cor. 8; 10:23-33, Rom. 14). This meant, specifically for Paul, that the practice of the early church in terms of the roles allotted to women should not violate this principle anymore than should speaking in tongues or prophesying. We cannot therefore understand 1 Corinthians 14:34 ("Let the women keep silent. . .") without regard for both the social context of the early church and Paul's general premises.

Too often, however, such general statements are pushed aside, while the specific statements are seen as the more important. Yet it is the general principles which must guide us in understanding the assumptions behind the specific instructions. To understand an author fully is to appreciate the interplay which takes place between his general principles and the specific situations in which he must apply them. This type of clue helps us evaluate the scope intended by the author and prevents us from applying a passage in ways not intended. (See 4.1.)

8.3 *General Context*

Consideration must be given as well to the general intellectual and cultural situation within which the writer wrote. This affects, for example, the type of problems that the writer will treat. Paul did not confront issues such as genetic engineering, nuclear testing, or overpopulation. If we look in the Bible for specific references dealing with these and many other problems, we will, of course, be disappointed. This does not mean that we cannot use the Bible as a guide in issues on which it is silent. But it does mean that we will have to go behind the surface to the deeper principles which guided the biblical authors in their writing.

We must also realize that the range of answers available to an author is limited by the times in which he lived. Paul's culture did not allow him the option of recommending Gelusil for Timothy's stomach problems (1 Tim. 5:23). Perhaps he felt he had no other good options than to recommend wine. Today, however, most pastors would recommend that he see a doctor! If we are to do justice to Paul's specific ethical instructions, we must keep in mind that he was solving concrete problems with the options available to him. Thus when new options become available to the church in the course of history, they must be considered. The old options should not be chosen just because they were chosen once.

Paul also recommended a certain demeanor of women vis-a-vis men in worship or in marriage. But when other socially accepted options become available for male-female roles in the church, they should not be rejected out of hand for the reason that Paul did not choose them. *Decisions have contexts and they must be understood in those contexts.*

Likewise decisions involve certain ramifications in their context, but when the contexts change, the implications of the original decision change. A decision which was valid in a certain situation may no longer be valid in another situation in which the decision may have quite different effects. For instance, when Paul writes, in Romans 13, of the Christians' obedience to the state, the situation was much different from ours today. The context of this passage is Paul's teaching on Christian love (see the end of chapter 12 and 13:8-10), which would seem in many ways to be the antithesis of the state's use of power, especially in war. How then could Paul mix these two teachings together? One answer might be that in the context of Paul's time, the Christians to whom he was writing were not subject to the draft, and thus this type of obligation to support the state's violence did not enter into his consideration. Consequently, when the situation changes, and this *does* become a requirement of the state, another decision may very well be called for. To carry out an unqualified obedience to the state in this matter may indeed be applying the passage in a way not intended.

Another aspect of the general context is that biblical writers either shared or assumed for purposes of communication many of the commonplace assumptions held in their culture, which are no longer held to be true. For example, in Jude 14, we find Jude quoting 1 Enoch, a book which is found neither in the Hebrew Old Testament nor in the Apocrypha, but in the pseudepigrapha, which is a group of books whose authors, rather than writing in their own names, put the words in the mouths of some famous ancient figure, such as Enoch or Moses, so that their writings would get a better hearing. Today, of course, we know that 1 Enoch was not really written by Enoch, seventh from Adam, who lived before the Flood. But in Jude's time, evidently it was assumed that he was the writer. [1]

A similar type of observation can be made concerning the New Testament writers' use of the Old Testament. The way the Bible is used by these writers reflects the way that people in their culture generally used Scripture. One favorite method in that time was what we call *proof-texting,* without paying too much attention to what the passage actually meant in its original context. For example, Matthew, who is very concerned to present Jesus as the Messiah promised in the Old Testament, presents a series of incidents surrounding Jesus' birth which he sees as fulfilling Scripture. In one of these, Matthew 2:14, 15, we find a quotation from Hosea 11:1—Jesus' descent to Egypt and return being a fulfillment of the passage in Hosea. However, if we look up Hosea 11:1, we find it is part of a survey of Israel's history and concerns the exodus from Egypt, not a prediction about the future. The issue here for us is not whether Jesus was the Messiah. It is rather whether in this case we need to accept Matthew's proof-texting approach—a way of arguing which he learned from and shared with his contemporaries.[2]

Or again, a Greek translation, the Septuagint, was often quoted rather than the Hebrew text by New Testament writers. This explains why some quotations in the New Testament are not the same as the Old Testament verse when we look them up. A well-known example is Matthew 1:23—

'The virgin will conceive and bear a son, and he shall be called Emmanuel', a name which means 'God is with us' (NEB).

—which quotes Isaiah 7:14. In Matthew, the word *virgin* is used because that is the word used in the Greek of the Septuagint. In Isaiah, the specific word for *virgin* is not used:[3]

A young woman is with child, and she will bear a son, and will call him Immanuel (NEB).

Should we base our understanding of the Old Testament passage on a translation rather than on the Hebrew original just because some of the biblical writers apparently did so in order to communicate to their contemporaries? Rather we would say that such things were part of the cultural furniture which was necessarily used to communicate the gospel and need not bind our understanding today. This is part of the cultural limitations which biblical authors shared with others in their time. Neither our knowledge nor our practice need necessarily be limited to one particular culture at one particular time.

8.4 *Linguistic Context*

Since the biblical writers shared with their audience regular "secular" language, we normally assume that words in a passage are being used in their normal or customary sense. In fact, this is a necessary assumption if their words were to make any sense, then or now. (See 2.1.) In doing this, it is very easy to forget that the Bible was not written in English, even in King James English, but mainly in Hebrew and Greek. In their usage of Hebrew and Greek words we assume that the biblical authors were using them according to the conventional usage of those languages. When we wish to recover the meaning of an author's words, we must be guided by the customary use of words in his language rather than our own. It is the way a word was normally used in that language that will set the usual boundaries for our inferences about what the word may mean in a specific passage. For example, we are very familiar with the word *create* which is used in Genesis 1:1 for the creation of the world. It is often assumed that this word means that God created something out of nothing. But before we can legitimately assume that Genesis 1:1 is talking about God making something out of nothing, we must ask whether this is a customary use of *bara*, "create," in the Bible. How would the writer's audience have understood the term in this context? We must seek to answer inductively, by examining how the word is used.

In Exodus and Numbers, the word *bara* is used for events in history—for God *doing* something, rather than *making* something:

Then God said, "Behold, I am going to make a covenant. Before all your people I will perform miracles which have not been *produced in all the earth* [literally, "created"] nor among any of the nations; and all the people among whom you live will see the working of the Lord, for it is a fearful thing that I am going to perform with you" (Ex. 34:10). (Italics added.)

"If these men die the death of all men, or if they suffer the fate of all men, then the Lord has not sent me. But if the Lord *brings about an entirely new thing* [literally, "creates"] and the ground opens up its mouth and swallows them up with all that is theirs, and they descend alive into Sheol, then you will understand that these men have spurned the Lord" (Num. 16:29, 30). (Italics added.)

Or again, in Psalms we find the following:

Create in me a clean heart, O God, and renew a steadfast spirit within me (51:10).

Thou dost send forth Thy Spirit, and they are *created;* and Thou dost renew the face of the ground (104:30). (Italics added.)

In Isaiah, the same word is used for God's action in "creating" Israel (43:1, 15). In none of these cases does it appear that God is making something out of nothing. Rather, he is renewing, sustaining, or transforming what already exists. In addition, if we would translate Genesis 1:1ff as the grammar would seem to indicate—"When God began to create the heavens and the earth, the earth being. . . . God said, 'Let there be light. . . ' "—we can readily see how the sense "transform" also fits its occurrence here.

This is not to say that there are not times when words are used in new or novel ways. In the Great Commission, for example, Jesus used the term *matheteuo*, "make disciples," in a unique way:

"Go therefore and *make disciples* of all the nations, baptizing them in the name of the Father and the Son and the Holy Spirit, teaching them to observe all that I commanded you; and lo, I am with you always, even to the end of the age" (Mt. 28:19, 20). (Italics added.)

Ordinarily in Greek, *matheteuo* seems to be used as an intransitive verb, that is, the action of the verb refers to the subject.[4] Used in this way, *matheteuo* would refer to a person deciding for himself to become a disciple of another. Jesus, however, does not follow this normal usage. He uses it in an active sense—that is, the subject of the verb is to make others become disciples. Thus the implications and the meaning of the verb are different. To understand this passage we need to unpack the significance of this change for the idea of discipleship. If we do our inductive study carefully, we will look for such clues on which to base ourselves and not assign words their meanings on the basis of what a passage means to us in our interpretive tradition.

8.5 *Conclusion*

The context into which words are put largely determines their meaning. It is thus vitally important for us to reconstruct the correct, authentic context for the biblical writings. Seen from this perspective, we can understand the words correctly.

Footnotes
1. This example is taken from Dewey M. Beegle, *Scripture, Tradition and Infallibility,* (Grand Rapids: Eerdmans, 1973), pp. 176-179.
2. Beegle, pp. 236-239.
3. *Betula* is the Hebrew for "virgin." In Isaiah 7:14, *na^{c}ara,* "young lady," is used, as the modern translations read.
4. Gerhard Kittel and Gerhard Friedrich, *Theological Dictionary of the New Testament,* vol. 4, (Grand Rapids, Mich.: Eerdmans, 1967).

9 | The Motivational Perspective

9.1 *Motivation*

From the composition and situation we can make some estimate as to the motivation of a statement. In the example discussed above from 1 Corinthians 14 ("Let the women keep silent. . ."), the motivation seems fairly clear. Paul wants to correct certain abuses of Christian freedom in the Corinthian church which were impeding their witness. What motivates is a desire to correct for the sake of the gospel, not a wish to set forth the ideal role of women in Christian worship. The very existence of the Christian church in Corinth was at stake, for if by their excessive display of freedom they alienated both the Jewish and the Gentile communities, it would reduce the ability of the church to reach new members and eventually bring about the end of the Christian church at Corinth.

Likewise in Amos 5 (see 4.1): Since the denouncement of Israelite worship is found in the context of his listing practices illustrating their social oppression on the one hand and his call for them to do justice and righteousness on the other, we are on the right track if we understand his motivation to be one of criticizing a wrong notion of worship rather than setting forth the ideal pattern of worship. The Israelites apparently thought God would forgive all and maintain His special relationship with them if the sacrificial system were maintained. Amos, on the contrary, argued that worship is ineffective—is unacceptable to God—when social injustice is rampant.

While the question of why someone wrote something is a very difficult one to answer, it is one of the most fruitful. Many passages with which we are very familiar take on a new life when seen from this perspective. Second Corinthians 5:14-17 is such a passage, especially verses 16, 17:

No longer, then, do we judge anyone by human standards. Even if at one time we judged Christ according to human standards, we no longer do so. When anyone is joined to Christ he is a new being; the old is gone, the new has come.

When we see that 2 Corinthians is written in the context of a struggle between Paul and some "super-apostles" at Corinth (2 Cor. 11:5), the verses take on a new dimension. These super-apostles were authoritarian, had the gift of speech, and were able to command monetary support from the Corinthians. Paul, on the other hand, was not so strong; he was not a powerful speaker; and he did not take monetary support from the Corinthians. Beside the powerful super-apostles, he was a sorry spectacle.

These super-apostles came with letters of recommendation (3:1), while Paul had only the Corinthians themselves (3:2). His letter was written in their hearts. The appeal, then, to a new way of judging people based on our relationship to Christ, speaks to the core of the matter. If the Corinthians have transformed minds, then they will not judge as the world judges, but instead will see Paul as the real apostle—in all his weakness. If they are not transformed, then they will judge as the world, claiming the super-apostles as their own and rejecting Paul.

In this light, we can understand Paul's motivation. We can understand why Paul would appeal to the Corinthians no longer to judge by human standards. His own apostleship is at stake. From a human point of view, Paul's life makes no sense. But from the perspective of people controlled by the love of Christ, Paul's life is the quintessence of good sense.

In general, it could be said that motivation is the single most useful key to understanding a passage but one of the most difficult to obtain. This is because what was motivating an author of long ago is not readily available for present-day study. It must often be determined by careful reconstruction of the circumstances surrounding the life of the author, especially those events close to the time of his writing the work we are studying, accompanied by a careful examination of the book—its structure, type, and contents.

9.2 Misunderstanding and Ambiguity

We have been discussing the clues available for making practical inferences concerning the meaning of a passage. But sometimes the clues are not enough. Since words can have various meanings depending on what an author has in mind, there are often several legitimate ways to understand a passage—several ways to "take" a statement. This uncertainty is called *ambiguity*. Ambiguity leads to misunderstanding when we choose a legitimate meaning for a passage but one which is not what the author intended. Misunderstanding does not usually arise from not knowing the meaning of words, but rather from understanding words in a "correct" way, but in a way not intended by the author.

Because language is by nature ambiguous, it should not surprise us to find statements in the Bible which, in spite of our study, may remain ambiguous. Sometimes it is because of their terseness, sometimes because we can no longer recover the tacit dimension due to our lack of knowledge. One such statement, for example, is Jesus' reply to those who questioned Him on the matter of paying taxes: "Render to Caesar the things that are Caesar's; and to God the things that are God's" (Mt. 22:21). The meaning of this passage has been debated endlessly. Recently I heard a careful exegetical paper on this and related passages. The author suggested that it would be very helpful to know the intonation pattern that Jesus used in uttering this statement, especially whether the emphasis had been placed on the first or last half of the saying. When the meeting was opened for discussion, one person asked why it had taken the speaker so many pages and so much time to comment on such a short passage, since Jesus needed very few words to say what He wanted to say—that is, that we should pay taxes (in other words, Americans should pay their income taxes and not withhold a percentage as a protest against high military spending, which was the question under discussion). Furthermore, since this was perfectly clear from the text, we did not have to worry about the inflectional pattern that Jesus might have used.

While such an answer may appeal to us for its simplicity, we can recognize what has happened. The respondent has used his own assumptions for understanding the saying. Since he evidently pays American income taxes and believes others should pay them as well, when he finds a statement of Jesus' saying "Render to Caesar the things that are Caesar's," what could be more logical than to conclude that Jesus was commanding Americans to pay income tax? What the reader of the paper had been attempting to do, however, was to reconstruct Jesus' assumptions (the tacit dimension). What taxes were they talking about—religious taxes, civil taxes, taxes to the Roman government, to local government, etc.? What were they used for, and what were the issues at stake? Was it a test to see if Jesus was a Zealot? All of this must be taken into account if we are to take Jesus' teachings seriously. Now it may well be that in texts like this one, because of their ambiguity, we will not be able to arrive at a consensus as to the meaning the author intended. (In fact, Jesus may have wished to answer in such an enigmatic way so that they could not accuse Him of anything. It has been suggested to me that we should understand this as Jesus' press conference—and construe His remarks accordingly.) But, hopefully, we can disagree on the basis of evidence and practical inferences which are open to discussion.

I do not want to say that the writer of the paper described above was right nor that the person who objected was wrong. What I want to illustrate are some of the pitfalls to which we all too easily succumb when we try to leap the chasm from the Bible to our present practice. The more important the issue is for us personally, the harder it is for us to consider things carefully. It is especially hard to admit that our bases in Scripture do not always support us as clearly as we might think they do.

9.3 *Probable and Possible*

Since there are many possible interpretations that a passage could conceivably have, the task of careful Bible study is to reduce the possible meanings to the most probable one. Some people seem to feel that if a passage *could* have meant something, then it *must* mean that, or at least that must be one of its legitimate meanings. It is surprising how often people are concerned only with deriving a possible meaning, without going any further. How often have you heard someone ask, "Well, couldn't it mean that?" The question to be asked instead is, '*Why* should we think it means that?' We must ask for evidence and the practical inferences that get from the evidence to their interpretation. There is a great difference between what a passage could mean and what it does mean; between credulity and faith, misguided sincerity and careful study.

9.4 *Summary*

To understand a passage is to determine the actual meaning its author intended. To gain this goal, we must uncover the tacit dimension underlying it. Since this dimension is never open to direct observation, it must be gotten at indirectly through the clues of composition, situation and motivation. From these clues and by exercising the powers of empathy, we make practical inferences as to what the author reasonably intended. At times we will not have enough evidence. Then, since the tacit dimension will not be as clear as we need for an unambiguous understanding, there will be several possible interpretations. In these cases we must sift the various possibilities to find the most *probable* interpretation.

PART V | **Understanding as Change**

"How can we take a popular man like this, a folk hero practically, and say he isn't good enough to be a priest? That is an insult to the common man."

"Many would applaud the dismissal," said the professor of moral theology. "After all, your common man knows he threw away a fortune in baseball."

"What of the reputation of the diocese when he begins to teach and preach?" said Father Pomeroy. "What, when he tells people that what they believe and what they do are the same thing?"

Klise, The Last Western

10 | Significance and Change

10.1 *Significance*

In chapter 4, we made the distinction between what a speaker means when he says something, and the meaning the statement may have for the audience. (See 4:2.) The former we called *meaning* while the latter we termed *significance.* In previous chapters we have been concerned with *meaning*—how we understand another when he speaks or writes. In this chapter we will devote ourselves to the *significance* of a statement—in what ways the Bible is meaningful to us today.

While the meaning of a passage in Scripture depends on an author and his context, the significance of a passage depends on *our* situation. When I was in graduate school, the first course I took in Bible was a study of Deuteronomy. When we came to chapter 14 containing the regulations concerning clean and unclean animals, I worked through it very rapidly, thinking there was little significance in it. But when we spent time on the passage in class, I found that for the professor, as well as for the rest of the class, the passage had a good deal of significance, since some very basic practices in Jewish life were at issue.

The major problem in finding the significance of a passage is that it may vary from individual to individual, and from context to context. Thus, while the meaning of a statement remains constant, its significance changes. In fact, it may be different for different people or situations at the same time. For example, Paul set forth a principle in 1 Corinthians: "All things are lawful for me, but not all things are profitable" (1 Cor. 6:12a). Although Paul may be quoting from the Corinthians themselves here, he goes on to show how this principle has several quite different applications. Its significance in the area of food is that all food may be eaten (as opposed, perhaps, to the Jewish distinctions between clean and unclean food). In the area of sexual morality, however, it does make a difference how one's appetites are satisfied. Union with a prostitute is forbidden. Thus the statement had at least two quite different applications for Paul and for the Corinthian church.

The implication of this is that there is no mechanical way to automatically derive significance from meaning. There are too many variables. This does not mean that understanding the meaning of a statement is immaterial to discovering its significance. Meaning must precede significance as induction precedes deduction. To apply a passage properly, we must first determine its meaning as accurately as we are able.

The other half of this coin is that because we find a statement significant in some way is no indication that we have found either its actual meaning or its proper application. (See chapter 1.) In the following paragraphs we would like to discuss some of the guides we need to follow in getting from meaning to application.

10.2 Implication and Analogy

One way we have of determining the significance of a passage is by applying the principle of analogy—what would be our cultural counterparts to the situation to which the passage speaks? For example, in Amos 5:20-24, Amos contrasts the people's worship—their assemblies, sacrifices, etc.—with God's desire for social justice. (See 4.1.) It was the demand for social justice that took precedence over the acts of religious piety. In today's setting the analogous setting would be the church and its worship. The question that needs to be addressed to the church is the relationship between divine worship and social justice. For example, one could ask if voting patterns of church members were for or against programs which are concerned with justice and equality for the poor.

A second way we have of judging the application of a passage is to note its implications. In 1 Corinthians 8, Paul writes about meat offered to idols. Although in principle it would be harmless to eat such food, in cases where this would cause offense to someone of weaker faith or conscience, Paul suggested refraining from eating such meat. The implication would be that even where there is nothing wrong with a certain practice, if it would offend a fellow Christian to the point of causing him or her to waver in the faith, it is best to abstain. For example, when I visit our Hopi Christian brothers and sisters in Arizona, I, as a tourist, might want to attend some of the dances which have religious significance for the Hopi. These dances are harmless as far as I am concerned, and I would be a spectator along with other tourists. But for some Hopi Christians, Christianity is a repudiation of the Hopi religion and its ceremonies. For me to attend might be seen as giving a stamp of approval to these "pagan" ceremonies. It would be better for me to forgo the ceremonies than to cause any harm that might result.

In another setting the application might be different. In a traditional Mennonite community where the use of alcoholic beverages is frowned upon, an individual who sees no problem in their moderate consumption might abstain entirely for the sake of others' consciences. (This is not to argue that, in fact, drinking is neutral—but rather to suggest that one who so considers it, might abstain for the reason cited.) For as Paul writes in 1 Corinthians 8:13:

> So then, if food makes my brother sin, I will never eat meat again, so as not to make my brother fall into sin (TEV).

10.3 *Active Definitions*

Besides using the principles of analogy and implication, a third way in which we can determine the significance and application of a passage for today is to construct *active definitions*. An *active definition* is a way of defining a concept by its observable manifestations—that is, by actions that can be seen in real life. For example, let us take the concept of our love for God. This is a fairly abstract concept—love is an internal emotion or feeling, and God is not materially present. In 1 John, however, we find an active definition of such love:

> If someone says he loves God, but hates his brother, he is a liar. For he cannot love God, whom he has not seen, if he does not love his brother, whom he has seen (1 Jn. 4:20, TEV).

As a first step toward constructing an active definition, John says one's love for God can be tested by how one loves his fellowman. But love for fellowman, like love for God, is also a vague concept. Many people express love in different ways. John again helps us by providing an active definition for this love:

> If a rich person sees his brother in need, yet closes his heart against his brother, how can he claim that he loves God? My children, our love should not be just words and talk; it must be true love, which shows itself in action (1 Jn. 3:17, 18, TEV).

Here the active definition is complete—love for God can be observed in the act of meeting the material needs of the poor brother.

While these three processes of implication, analogy, and active definition can aid us in determining the significance of a passage, it needs to be stressed that this is no mechanical process. It may take a good bit of discernment to arrive at an accurate assessment of what a proper application would be. In addition, there are a series of hindrances which at times make it difficult for us to find a passage's proper application.

10.4 *Significance and Relativity*

We have shown above (see chapter 8) that meaning is heavily dependent on the context within which something is said or written. This in turn influences the significance that a statement has for us. When the situation changes so that the tacit assumptions of a statement are no longer valid, then the significance changes. For example, in Matthew 19:28 when Jesus says to His disciples, ". . . when the Son of Man will sit on His glorious throne, you also shall sit upon twelve thrones, judging the twelve tribes of Israel," one of the twelve whom Jesus addressed was Judas. But in light of what happened later, we do not expect to see Judas sitting on one of the twelve thrones. Perhaps the significance of this statement for us has more to do with how Judas, who had so much to gain, could lose it all, than it does with Judas's position in heaven.

This principle has its most immediate effect on how we carry out specific instructions. For instance, we find in 1 Corinthians 16:20 the exhortation, "Greet one another with a holy kiss." We know from the rest of Paul's letter that the Corinthian church was rent with factions and internal strife. It would be fitting, then, at the end of the letter to such a church to urge them to greet one another in a friendly way as prescribed by their culture. In present-day America, however, such a practice is obviously not the usual greeting used to indicate friendliness between men. An Amishman was once brought into a psychiatric clinic by his friends. As they left him, they all kissed him good-by. The psychiatrist, observing this, began his analysis with the observation that the man had obvious homosexual tendencies! The "holy kiss," which had one intent and significance in one culture, has quite another implication in another culture. Perhaps in our day a hearty handshake would be a better equivalent. This example has perhaps more to do with cultural relativity than with the interpretation of language; however the two are very closely intertwined, since language reflects its culture and is, in fact, part of human culture. As part of human culture, it too is bound by its situation. *When the cultural situation changes, the significance of the Scripture changes.*

Since Scripture was given in a variety of contexts, all Scripture cannot be blended into one context so that every verse is made to say the same thing as every other verse on a subject. We do a grave disservice to an author if we make him say the same things as every other author who has written on the subject in the Bible. The fact that God moved people in various times and in diverse circumstances should warn us against trying to read everything "flat" without the benefit of its background. The word of God comes to people in human history and shares the relativity of that history. Thus more than one word may be necessary on the subject. We, in turn, must be aware of this multiplicity, a multiplicity which will trouble us only if the historical aspect of revelation is not properly understood.

We have ample evidence of this historical conditioning of the word of God in the Bible itself. For example, in Isaiah's time the word of God through Isaiah was that Jerusalem would not fall, and the temple would not be destroyed (2 Kings 19:32). About a century later, Jeremiah the prophet predicted that in his time the city and the temple would be destroyed (Jer. 7:1-15). His opponents practically lynched him for saying this (26:1-24), for they, like Isaiah, predicted that God would save Jerusalem and the yoke of the kingdom of Babylon would be broken (28:1-4). It was these latter prophets however, who were the false prophets, for they were repeating the old word of the Lord in changed circumstances. When we try to determine the significance of God's word for us today, we must realize that there may be several messages from several times. Rather than reducing the witness to one, we must allow the Bible to speak to us in all its shades and hues. To keep on repeating a single line which was true once will be to become a false prophet in new circumstances.

Jesus himself used this type of approach in understanding the Scriptures in His day. When questioned about divorce (Mark 10:2-9), He asked His questioners about what was in the law. Knowing the provisions made in the law for divorce, they quoted from Deuteronomy 24. Now, in quoting the law, they were quoting from what was the heart of the divine revelation to them, from the very words of God given to Moses himself. But in reply, Jesus stated that it was because of the hardness of their hearts that God gave them this command. (We might say because of human weakness or fallibility.) Jesus was not content to merely say what the text says but tried instead to lay bare the tacit dimension—*why* such a command was given to those people in that time. By asking the *why* question, Jesus was in a position to go beyond their immediate concern with how to apply Deuteronomy 24 in His day, to what was the significance of the passage in terms of what else was found in Scripture. He suggested that since the law in Deuteronomy 24 was given because of the people's hardness of heart, it therefore did not represent God's ultimate ideal on the matter of marriage. He then quoted the Creation accounts in Genesis 1 and 2 as a description of how man and woman should relate in marriage. Thus, in determining the application of Scripture, we must always ask, "What else does Scripture say on this matter?"

10.5 *Letter and Spirit*

A constant temptation which confronts us in trying to make the Bible relevant in our lives today is to find its significance in keeping the rules and regulations we find in it. We somehow feel if we do exactly as the Bible teaches in specific instances, we will be true to it *in toto*. It is sometimes easier to apply Scripture blindly than to consider what its motivation might be. It often takes less thought to live by the letter than to be led by the spirit behind the letter.

The problem with such an approach is that it can never be exact enough or exhaustive enough to transfer all the rules and regulations into modern life. For Christians, this is especially true of those rules in the Old Testament. In Leviticus 19, for example, we find both the instruction to love one's neighbor, which we consider very important, and the instruction to refrain from wearing garments made of two kinds of thread, which (Orthodox Jews excepted) is not practiced anymore. Not even all the instructions for Gentile believers in the New Testament are practiced in our time. One thinks of the instructions in Acts 15 prohibiting the eating of things that have been strangled and of blood. Or again, one thinks of Paul's dress code for women in 1 Timothy 2:9 which includes among the forbidden things, "braided hair." Even the most pious Christian women do not feel bound by this directive today. Thus a new legalism based on either the Bible as a whole or the New Testament in particular is bound to fail, for it will need to devise some principle of its own for selecting what it does consider appropriate for today's practice. In the end, people will pick and choose what they consider appropriate to practice.

We must realize that *the customs and norms of one historical period are not necessarily more appropriate to Christianity than those of another,* even if they be those of first-century Palestine or sixteenth-century Europe. We must be guided by the significance of specific practices in their historic context, rather than absolutizing them. For example, the life of Jesus is often presented as embodying ideas that ought to guide us as Christians. Yet there is much about the life of Jesus that is, in fact, quite insignificant in terms of our Christian lives today. The way He dressed, the language He spoke, His occupation, even His itinerant life-style are seen as inapplicable by most Christians. Similarly, the assumption that He never married is usually not considered binding. These facts are seen as either peculiar to Him, or as cultural accidents, due to the fact that He lived in first-century Palestine. His examples of suffering and servanthood, however, are considered to be binding for Christians today. How, then, do we differentiate the significant from the culturally conditioned? It is a question of intent. Wherein was Christ laying down an example for His followers? Here we can be guided in part by His own words, as in Mark 10:43-45 where He linked His ministry as servant with how and what His disciples are to be and do.

The position of the Apostle Paul, who struggled with the problem of the application of law to Christianity, may help us. For Paul, it was not that the law no longer had validity for the Christian—note how often he quotes the Old Testament to support his teachings (far oftener than he quotes Jesus, in fact)—but close adherence to law alone is not sufficient, since the aim of law still will not be met by this. The law has its place, not adhered to for the sake of the letter, but rather as an example whose spirit is to be applied to changing contexts. Likewise for us, close adherence even to the New Testament teachings will not encompass for us the intentions of the New Testament. We are not against law any more than Paul was, but the law should be a guide rather than a master.

Christians are showing a misguided veneration for the Bible when they try to "freeze" its specific, culturally bound statements as the message of the Bible for today. At best this practice manifests itself as a mild form of legalism and cultural conformity—not to our own culture, to be sure, but a conformity nevertheless. Was not this, in fact, a problem of interpretation Jesus spoke to in His own day when He said, "Woe to you, scribes and Pharisees, hypocrites! For you tithe mint and dill and cumin, and have neglected the weightier provisions of the law: justice and mercy and faithfulness; but these are the things you should have done without neglecting the others" (Mt. 23:23). Christ would have us live in the spirit of the the law rather than be slaves to the letter of the law at the expense of the spirit. Note well that Jesus condemns neither the law nor these specific practices—rather He denounces getting wrapped up in the minutiae of practices at the expense of general principles. [1]

Footnotes
1. Often because of our preconceived notions about Judaism in the time of Christ, we read these passages with an anti-Semitic bias. This has led to the most unfortunate consequence both in history and today. Indeed this has fostered both a misunderstanding of Judaism as "legalism" and an overlooking of our own Christian forms of legalism. In Jesus' time as today, Judaism was a living, lively, and vibrant religion—based on God's grace and the privilege of participating in God's eternal purposes for human destiny. On the other hand, in the church, historically as well as now, there are legalists who see religion as living by rules without a real notion of the love of God for people and His grace to them. Legalism knows no religious boundaries.

11 | The Significance of the Bible as God's Word

11.1 *Authority*

The significance which the Bible has for us today is necessarily bound with its authority. For the Bible becomes authoritative as we faithfully seek its significance for us.[1] Conversely, it ceases to be an authority when we no longer allow it this function. Dr. Spock's book on child care is an "authority" for parents in the sense that they read it to find out what to do in taking care of an infant. If they only read it but do not follow it, Dr. Spock would not be authoritative for them. He might be quoted as an authority on the subject, but it would be an abstract authority, since in practice what he says makes little difference. From this analogy we can see that authority does not depend on whether people understand a book, but on whether it makes some difference in the way they act.

This functional view of authority is quite different from the more usual approach in which the Bible is held to be authoritative because of some quality which it has—for example, God inspired it, it is without error, etc. It is much safer to debate authority in these abstract terms, making it a matter of holding to a set of definitional statements about the nature of the Bible, than it is to take it authoritatively in terms of obedience to its teachings. It is not what we believe about the Bible—as if inspiration and authority are something we bestow upon it—but what the Bible *is* for us that gives it its authority (Mt. 7:21-23).

For Bible study, another danger with defining authority in abstract terms is that it rests on deduction, usually beginning with some theological premise. Once a premise is accepted as true and applied deductively, then the whole inductive process is short-circuited. If, for example, it is held that there are no errors of any kind in the Bible (a claim which the Bible does not make for itself), then any inductive study which finds such errors is "wrong"—since it has already been said that there are none. (This statement should not be understood as saying there are errors. What is meant is that any such statement only be made *after* a careful inductive study, *not before*.)[2]

This approach, of course, is another way of finding in the Bible exactly what we want to find. Far from upholding the authority of the Bible, those who use this approach actually make the Bible subservient to the authority of their own theological dogmas. But since the authority of the Bible stands above the authority of dogmas, it is our inductive, empirical study of the Bible which must pass judgment on these dogmas, not the other way around.

11.2 *Canon*

The Bible is referred to as the *canon,* and the process of deciding which books belong in the Bible is referred to as the process of *canonization.* The term canon has the sense of "measuring" or of a "measuring stick." *Canon* thus reflects the normative role of the Bible in the Christian faith; that is, it is the measuring stick against which all else is measured. The writings which belong in the canon are those that both measure up to this task and can serve as a measure for others.

The process of writings finding their way into the body of Scripture— canonization—was a historical one that took place, for the New Testament, over a three-hundred-year period. It was not until toward the end of the fourth century A.D. that the church came to a rough agreement on which books were Scripture and which were not. Even then there was no universal agreement. Our present New Testament, then, reflects the experience of the early church. It contains those books which, in those beginning centuries of the church, stood the test of time and faith. In a way, the process is much like that of a book becoming a literary classic. It must endure and be found worthy by a succession of generations. The canon, in a like manner, represents the books that "measured"—were found most useful in the life of the church. It does not represent a group of books imposed on the church by dogma.

At a certain stage dogmatic considerations did enter in. For example, the criterion of apostolic authorship was required. Because of this demand, the Book of Hebrews had difficulty gaining universal acceptance into the canon. When, however, people generally agreed that Paul wrote it, it was included. In this case the desire for the book to be Scripture seems to have preceded its being given the right credentials at a later stage. Today, however, few would hold to Pauline authorship.

We can see now how the functional view of the Bible's authority discussed in the previous section has its roots in the historical process of canonization. It was because of the function of these books in the lives of people and in the faith of the church that they became included in the canon and therefore normative for Christian faith and life. It is what these books *did* for people, not people's beliefs about them, that made them Scripture.

The idea of the canon underlines a core concept of this work: that the meaning of the biblical material is determinate and constant, while the significance is variable. (See 4.2.) To proclaim something as a standard is to claim that it is something which in some sense does not change. For instance, in the United States, the foot, the pound, and other measurements are all measured against a standard which is carefully preserved in a controlled environment. This is done to insure that there is no deviation—because as a standard it must always be the same. Thus, to proclaim a book as a standard is to say that the meaning in some real way does not change; it is determinate.

But it has this authority as a standard only as it finds application in life—as we find it significant for us in our situation. This significance keeps changing constantly since the situation to which we make application keeps changing. Thus there is stability and change in our understanding of the Bible. When we lose either pole of this process of understanding, the canon ceases to function for us as a canon—the measure of our faith and life.

11.3 *Inspiration*

The verses that are usually referred to concerning inspiration are 2 Timothy 3:16, 17 (TEV):

All Scripture is inspired by God [*or,* Every Scripture inspired by God] and is useful for teaching the truth, rebuking error, correcting faults, and giving instruction for right living, so that the person who serves God may be fully qualified and equipped to do every kind of good deed.

The emphasis in this verse is on the *function* of the Word—its utility—not on its abstract nature. It defines inspiration in active terms—what it can do, not what it is. Views of inspiration which go beyond this usually owe more to the theological or philosophical presuppositions of their adherents than they do to the Bible's own teaching. From the standpoint of this verse, it seems clear that inspiration means that the written Word which we call Scripture is adequate to communicate what is necessary for us to function as we should. Thus inspiration affirms the adequacy of human language and in particular the language that we find in the Bible as a vehicle for revelation. Inspiration should *not* (contrary to much that is said) be used to support one's views either about the content of revelation or about the way in which the Bible can or should be understood.

For example, the concept of *verbal plenary inspiration,* claims that the whole, as well as each word, is inspired. But as a view of inspiration, it can not legitimately tell us ahead of time what content these inspired words should communicate to us, nor the type of language used to do this. It cannot tell us, for example, whether the words are to be taken historically or parabolically. When people do so in the name of verbal plenary inspiration—or any other view of inspiration for that matter—they are going beyond the doctrine of inspiration to a doctrine of revelation, a doctrine which tells what *type* of information God reveals. On this latter point, the content of revelation, we can either proceed inductively— study the text to see what it means—or we can proceed deductively— define it in terms of dogma and then manipulate the text to fit our dogmas about it. It is the latter that is all too often done. When this is done, battles are frequently fought about inspiration, which, strictly speaking, have nothing to do with inspiration but have to do rather with people's views *about* the Bible.

A classic case of this is confusing inspiration and authorship. In the example just given above, some would feel uncomfortable with the claim that Paul did not write Hebrews. This would seem to be a challenge to inspiration. If we examine this feeling a bit, we can see that, in fact, it rests on a faulty argument. The inspiration of a book does not rest on its human authorship. If this were true, then inspiration would be due to the quality of certain individuals, not due to God's moving (2 Pet. 1:21). Furthermore, to claim that Paul did not write Hebrews is not to deny the effectiveness of Hebrews. Suppose, for example, that it were discovered that the frescoes in the Sistine Chapel were not painted by Michaelangelo—would that make them any less beautiful? Of course not. We would just have discovered another great creative genius. Likewise with the Bible, to attribute different authorship than that traditionally assigned is just to recognize another writer of inspired literature. It is not to deny inspiration of the work.

Not only can inspiration not prejudge the content or authorship of Scripture, it cannot define for us a method of understanding. It does, however, assure us that the words used are adequate to their task of communicating the meaning.[3] It is up to us to develop the best methods we can to understand the meaning of the words. The following diagram may help to clarify this:

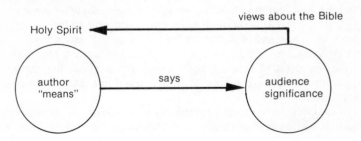

views about the Bible

Holy Spirit ◄

author
"means"

says

audience
significance

From this diagram we can see that when we impose our views about the Bible onto the Bible, we are in a sense telling God what and how He can communicate! Rather, we are to use inductive processes to put the passage in perspective so we can understand what, in fact, is being communicated.

11.4 *The Christocentric Interpretation of the Bible*

One of the more troublesome aspects of interpretation for Christians is the relationship between the Old Testament and the New Testament. We do not want to develop a position on this here, but only to see how our understanding of the nature of language relates to it. We have noted that meaning rests on the intentions in the mind of an author. An implication of this is that what an author's words mean must make sense within his historical horizon within his specific context. As we have seen, meaning is, in fact, bound to context.

It is true, of course, that people sometimes say more than they mean. The reverse is also true. When someone makes a statement which turns out to have more importance, more implications, than was initially apparent, we say that the person meant more than was said. But we must be careful to analyze accurately what happens in these cases. First of all, if the author of such a statement is asked about it, he or she might well reply, "I didn't realize at the time what a significant statement I was making, but I guess I did mean that by implication." Two things should be stressed. First, the statement, as well as its implications, makes sense—has meaning—in terms of the original historical context and author. Secondly, in talking about the significance of a statement, we are not discussing its original meaning. Language does not have some mystical surplus of meaning of which the author was unaware, and which does not make sense in context, but which is discovered only later, independent of the original author and context.

From this perspective we can now understand how a Christocentric interpretation of the Bible makes sense. This is not a way of understanding the Bible; it is not a principle of understanding language; rather it is a way of evaluating significance. To understand the Old Testament we need to see it from the perspective of the authors, in its literary and historical perspective. To determine the *significance*, we must see it in the perspective of Jesus Christ. The statement is frequently made that "Jesus is Lord of Scripture." From what we have seen, we know that the statement cannot correctly imply that Jesus gives us the *original intent* of the authors of the Bible. Rather, correctly seen, it must imply that our understanding of the *significance* of a passage takes Jesus as normative.

For example, in Genesis 3:15 (TEV) we read:

I will make you and the woman hate each other; her offspring and yours will always be enemies. Her offspring will crush your head, and you will bite their heel.

Church tradition has understood this verse as referring to Jesus and Satan. Strictly speaking, this is the significance—the meaningfulness which the church found here. This is surely not what the author meant nor how he was understood when he wrote these words.

This use of the Christocentric approach as the *way* to understand the meaning of the Old Testament rests on two mistaken notions. The first has to do with the New Testament authors' use of the Old Testament, and the implications of this for our exegesis today. [4] The second rests on our frequent misuse of the language in the Bible itself when we operate as if it could be understood apart from its author, in his particular circumstances. To do this, as we have seen, is to deny the nature of the vehicle through which God chose to reveal Himself to us.

Practically speaking, then, reading the new Testament is not a shortcut for understanding the Old. The Old Testament must be understood on its own terms. Furthermore, an understanding of the Old Testament used as a guide and a brake on our understanding of the New, is perhaps our best defense against making the New Testament over into our own image.

Footnotes

1. John Bright, *The Authority of the Old Testament,* (Grand Rapids: Baker Book House, 1975), pp. 24-27.

2. On the controversy surrounding this subject of whether there are errors of any type in the Bible, see the helpful discussion in J. C. Wenger, *God's Word Written,* (Scottdale: Herald Press, 1966) and D. Beegle, *Scripture, Tradition and Infallibility,* (Grand Rapids: Eerdmans, 1973).

3. "Only if the thought is verbally correct is the communication what it is intended to be. If the content of revelation is of God, its communication in writing obviously must ensure that it is given as God would have us receive it. In this case, writing communicates the content of revelation, and inspiration guarantees its veracity." Finlayson, quoted in Beekman and Callow, from C. F. Henry, *Revelation and the Bible,* (Grand Rapids: Baker Book House, 1967), pp. 345-346.

4. A recent helpful treatment of this topic is Richard Longenecker, *Biblical Exegesis in the Apostolic Period* (Grand Rapids: Eerdmans, 1975).

12 | The Study of the Bible in the Church

12.1 *The Holy Spirit and Reason*

Lay people often take a rather casual attitude toward the study of Scripture. This is partly due to a vagueness about the proper goal of Bible study. But it is also partly due to a tendency to think that since it is the Holy Spirit who interprets the text for each individual, no real effort is required by the person. This leads to what might be called an abuse of the Holy Spirit, for it is almost as if God is being tempted or tested to do something for us—make us understand the text—which we are unwilling to do for ourselves. The Holy Spirit may have prompted or called forth the statements in the Bible, but the message was "incarnated" in human language and mediated by a human mind. While the ultimate importance of a statement may reside with its ultimate author or prompter, God through the Holy Spirit, its actual meaning is to be found through an understanding of the human author of the statement. Thus the Holy Spirit will not magically provide us with the tacit dimension of a statement. The descriptive task is our part of the understanding process. We have already pointed out that the presence of the Holy Spirit invoked in support of an interpretation is never sufficient to guarantee its correctness. (See 1.3.) Thus biblical interpretation must never call for the sacrifice of reason in the name of the Holy Spirit. Our reason, in fact, is our single best guide to understanding.

What we know may not seem reasonable, but *how* we know it, must be. Sometimes people confuse these two. Since what is known in the Bible seems "unreasonable,"—for example, miracle stories—they conclude that the use of reason is a threat to Bible study. On the contrary, to understand a miracle story we need to use our mental powers—reason—but what we come to know and understand—the object of our knowledge—may be "unreasonable." Reason is necessary for under-standing. Once we abandon it, we are in the shifting sands of gamesmanship, where, as in the time of the judges, each is free to do what is right in his or her own eyes.

Because of the necessity of reason, it is possible for Jews, Christians, and atheists to work at the descriptive task, uncovering the tacit dimension of the Bible, with surprising agreement. The intent of the author is based on public evidence and practical inferences which can be discussed by everyone who wants to study and comprehend. Being a Christian does not automatically confer on one an understanding of the Bible, nor does it particularly guard against incorrect interpretations. It should, however, affect the seriousness with which a person undertakes his or her task. Here we find a great paradox in the lives of Christians— that something that is so important to understand is often taken so lackadaisically, sometimes even in the name of the Spirit.

The major role of the Holy Spirit in Bible study is in convicting us and enabling us to be faithful to what can be known about the text. The Holy Spirit does not serve as a substitute for our intellect and common sense, but He is the power of God with us to illuminate us in our walk and to strengthen us in our faithfulness. It is in ascertaining the *significance* of the text that the Spirit performs His most valuable role for us in the study of the Scripture. The more faithfully we do our descriptive task of finding the intentions of the text, the more we allow the Holy Spirit to lead us in our Christian life. The less we want to understand the Bible, the more we are content and firm in our traditional answers and opinions, the more we stifle the Spirit. *Careful, inductive, rational Bible study, far from being opposed to the Spirit, is the one best way we have of allowing both the text and the Spirit to speak to and guide us in life.*

12.2 *Intellectualism*

For some, this may raise the specter of intellectualism—the fear that only an intellectual or scholarly elite can understand the Bible. Since most do not belong to this elite yet understand the Bible sufficiently for salvation, a dichotomy is set up: intellectual, scholarly knowledge, which is irrelevant, if not dangerous, versus the practical simple knowledge which is necessary and sufficient for salvation.

Now this in many ways represents a false understanding. There is no necessary antithesis between "saving" knowledge and "scholarly" knowledge. Actually their function is somewhat different and comple-mentary. On the one hand, there is beginning knowledge—what it takes to get started in the Christian life. On the other hand, there is the knowledge of maturation and decision making in life. We should not dismiss this latter as unimportant or insignificant. The thief on the cross, we assume, had saving knowledge, although he knew nothing of Christ's resurrection and probably nothing of His teachings or His life, which are surely not insignificant matters. It would be an error, then, to equate saving knowledge with "necessary" knowledge, assuming other knowledge to be "unnecessary." As Jesus' parable of the soils illustrates, it is one thing to germinate a seed, but quite another to nourish it, enabling its continued growth and fruit bearing. (See 1.3.)

This polarizing of simple common understanding with scholarly understanding also shows a mistaken notion about understanding. As we have tried to illustrate in this work, understanding has two parts: The first is listening (our descriptive reconstruction of the author's intentions) while the second is the carrying out of these intentions in one's own life (the significance). This second aspect of the process depends not so much on thinking as on willing. For the Bible to be understood at any level involves both the mind and the will. It is here, however, that we all have a problem. For most of us "know" more than we are willing to do. This means that our problems in understanding may at times not be lack of knowledge, even scholarly knowledge, but lack of will. In this case, additional knowledge *does* become irrelevant, because no complete understanding is possible. But this does not mean that the knowledge itself is irrelevant, only that for us it cannot become healing knowledge until we are ready to act on it.

The problem remains, however, that some have a great deal more knowledge than others. Some can read Hebrew and Greek, some know the cultural contexts within which the Bible was written, etc. In a very real sense, these are luxuries which not everyone can enjoy since they call for a considerable investment in time and money. But the fact that these tools are not available to everyone does not mean that they should be rejected by the other members of the church. This would presuppose neither a proper view of the church, nor a responsible use of gifts within the church.

The church is often compared to a human body. As the body has many different members with different functions, so in the church different persons with different gifts exercise different functions. Some are teachers, some preachers. No one argues that because all are not preachers, none should be; or that because all are not excellent teachers, none should excel. Likewise, to reduce what should be known to a common denominator attainable by all, is to deny the nature of the church. The church must learn to use its scholars and their gifts for the maturity of its members.

This suspicion of knowledge which is not possessed by everyone is also based in part on a mistaken understanding of the fact that everyone can read and understand Scripture for himself. The original intention of this idea was to say that the church is not the only channel of understanding Scripture. Some have mistakenly taken it to mean that all believers understand the Bible equally well. The history of the Christian church, however, shows plainly that there were giants of understanding who have soared above others in their study of Scriptures. These have enriched the church and its individual members. It should cause no alarm today, then, if there is inequality of understanding. Each should strive for as great an understanding as he or she can achieve, always remaining open for learning from those with yet greater understanding.

12.3 *Knowledge and Faith*

A latent fear may yet remain that knowledge is dangerous. If people know, then they may lose faith. This is not necessarily true, of course. As a Bible teacher, I have observed that for many, to gain knowledge is to increase in faith; for some, to gain knowledge is to come to real faith for the first time.

This fear may presume a false notion of faith—that faith is a thing which can be gained or lost. Rather, it may be more helpful to think of faith as an attitude or mental action one has toward an object. Knowledge does not so much cause people to lose faith but to change what it is they have faith in. Supposing our children bring home a stray kitten and, believing it to be a male, they name it Sam. If Sam later gives birth to kittens, they do not love Sam less. They only have a more accurate understanding of who Sam is. So it is with the Bible. The more we learn about it, the more accurate is our understanding of the object of our faith.

It is interesting that when the stakes are high (the actual conduct of life) as they should be in Bible study, some people feel that certain types of knowledge should not be used. In other areas of life, where we have much at stake—buying a home, a new car, or insurance—we seek for all the information we can obtain, because we feel there is a correlation between being well informed and making a good decision. This is true in the Bible as well. *The best decisions as to the Bible's implications for our lives today are based on the best information available as to its meaning.*

Finally, some people feel that serious study of the Bible is dangerous because it may uncover something which will discredit the Bible, that the Bible, in fact, must be protected. Usually what this means is that it is people's ideas or beliefs *about* the Bible that must be protected (for example, that Paul wrote Hebrews), not the Bible. Unfortunately, many do not distinguish between *their* understanding of the Bible and understanding the Bible. Understanding the Bible may challenge people's views, and this is dangerous. What this means in practice, then, is that having a traditional, orthodox understanding is more important than actually understanding what the text says.

If the Bible is what we claim it is, then it should be able to withstand our inquiries. But more than this, the careful study of the Bible is in itself an act of respect, for it says that this is important material which must be taken very seriously. This is the theme of a recent novel by Chaim Potok, called *In the Beginning.* In the novel, David Lurie, a brilliant young Orthodox Jew decides to become a Bible scholar. Unlike his teacher, a Talmudist who has stayed within the Orthodox tradition, he says, "I will go wherever the truth leads me. It is secular scholarship, Rabbi; it is not the scholarship of tradition. In secular scholarship there are no boundaries and no permanently fixed views."

To this, his teacher replies, "Lurie, if the Torah cannot go out into your world of scholarship and return stronger, then we are all fools and charlatans. I have faith in the Torah. I am not afraid of truth." Later in the conversation he adds, "I am not bothered by questions of truth. I want to know if the religious world view has any meaning today. Bring yourself back an answer to that, Lurie. Take apart the Bible and see if it is something more today than the *Illiad* and the *Odyssey.* Bring yourself back that answer, Lurie. Do not bring yourself back shallowness. . . ."[1]

Knowledge, in the end, is dangerous, not to the Bible, but to ourselves. When boundaries are no longer fixed, when traditions are no longer accepted just because they always have been, we will be forced to change. We may need to give up our cherished opinions. For this reason we do not always want to hear. But knowledge is only dangerous because truth confronts and demands change. If we would understand the Bible, we must change.

Footnotes
  1 Chaim Potok, *In the Beginning* (New York: Alfred A. Knopf, Inc., 1975), p. 435; used by permission.

Selected Bibliography

A Guide for Further Reading

In the following bibliography I have listed a limited number of books according to general theme or topic. Hopefully this can serve as a guide for those wishing to do additional reading connected with the major thesis raised in this book. I have especially tried to include work of a theoretical nature to complement the practical design of the present work.

I. Since a discussion of understanding language should be predicated on some grasp of the nature and function of language, the following works on semantics are basic to our theme. These works can roughly be divided into two, although overlapping, categories—those written from the standpoint of linguistics, and those written from the viewpoint of philosophy.

    A. Linguistic semantics

        1. Beekman, John and Callow, John. *Translating the Word of God.* Grand Rapids, Mich.: Zondervan, 1974. Linguistic semantics applied to understanding and translating the Bible.

        2. Leach, Geoffrey. *Semantics.* Gretna, La.: Pelican Books, 1974. A substantial work, integrating linguistics and semantics. As an introductory part followed by an advanced section.

        3. Lyons, J. *Structural Semantics.* Forest Grove, Oreg.: Blackwells, 1963. An introduction to an applied semantics—the understanding of language in a text.

—*Introduction to Theoretical Linguistics.* New York: Cambridge University Press, 1968. A complementary work to that above; deals with language theory.

4. Nilsen, Don L. F. and Alleen Pace Nilsen. *Semantic Theory: A Linguistic Perspective.* Rowley, Mass.: Newbury House Publishers, 1975. An introductory survey of semantics from the perspective of contemporary linguistic theory.

5. Palmer, F. R. *Semantics, A New Outline.* New York: Cambridge University Press, 1976. A brief, concise guide for the beginner to semantic theory.

B. Philosophical Semantics

1. Alston, William P. *Philosophy of Language.* London: Prentice-Hall, 1964. A brief introduction to the philosophy of language.

2. Searle, John R. *Speech Acts: An Essay in the Philosophy of Language.* New York: Cambridge University Press, 1969. A full-blown philosophical treatment of how language works. This is heavy, but rewarding reading. A standard bibliographical item in this area.

3. Schaff, Adam. *Language and Cognition.* New York: McGraw-Hill, translated 1973 (Polish, 1964). Treats linguistic relativity—do different languages demand different world views? His answer is no. The introduction by Noam Chomsky, one of the world's leading linguists, is by itself a concise rebuff of the Sapir-Whorf hypothesis.

4. Taylor, Daniel M. *Explanation and Meaning: An Introduction to Philosophy.* New York: Cambridge University Press, 1971. The second section of this book on meaning provides an introduction to the various ways philosophers have understood language to mean. May be easier reading for the beginner than Alston, although none of these works are easy.

II. While the preceding works are about understanding language, the following deal more particularly with the topic of hermeneutics—the study and interpretation of texts. Again, there are two categories: those with a more practical, empirical bent, taking a stance from within interpretational practice; and those of a more theoretical philosophical nature, which probe the understanding of understanding. The first category stands in spirit much closer to this work than the second. (See our statement on hermeneutics at the end of the Introduction.)

A. Practical hermeneutics

1. Funk, Robert W., Language, *Hermeneutics and Word of God.* New York: Harper & Row, 1966. Both a survey of the

'new hermeneutic' theology movement in Europe and an interpretation of specific texts.

2. Hirsch, E. D. *Validity in Interpretation.* New Haven, Conn.: Yale University Press, 1967. Written as an antidote to the "new criticism" which swept English literature. (For an introduction to this, see Warren, A. and Wellek, R., *Theory of Literature.* New York: Harcourt Brace, 1949).

   —*The Aims of Interpretation.* Chicago: University of Chicago Press, 1976. A collection of articles published to further elaborate and defend his arguments in *Validity in Interpretation.* This work should be read by all serious biblical exegetes and students of hermeneutics.

B. Theoretical hermeneutics

1. Achtemeier, Paul J. *An Introduction to the New Hermeneutic.* Philadelphia, Pa.: Westminster Press, 1969. A survey of this European theology, tracing it back to its philosophical roots. Has a valuable chapter on the nature of language. Surprisingly readable on such an obtuse topic.

2. Gadamer, Hans-Georg. *Truth and Method.* New York: Seabury Press, trans. 1975, (2nd German edition 1965). The translation of the major work of the leading philosopher of hermeneutics in Europe, while welcome, leaves something to be desired. Gadamer represents one pole of the present debate in hermeneutics—the philosophical presuppositions of understanding make objective understanding impossible—while Betti represents the other—the determining of validity and thus objective accuracy in understanding is essential to understanding. R. E. Palmer argues Gadamer's position, while Betti's is represented by E. D. Hirsch.

3. Palmer, Richard E. *Hermeneutics: Interpretation Theory in Schleirmacher, Disthey, Heidegger, and Gadamer.* Evanston, Ill.: Northwestern University Press, 1969. A general survey of hermeneutical theory reaching back to the Greeks and forward to modern thinkers. A follower of Gadamer, Palmer presents his view and an attack on Hirsch's views.

III. Traditionally the subject of biblical hermeneutics has included a treatment of the theological nature of the biblical text—revelation, inspiration, and associated topics. Our major focus has been on understanding the language of the text rather than its theological nature. Since entire books have been devoted to these topics, we would simply list several for those who wish to pursue these topics.

1. Beegle, Dewey M. *Scripture, Tradition and Infallibility.* Grand Rapids, Mich.: Eerdmans 1973 (earlier edition, *The Inspiration of Scripture,* 1963). A more lengthy treatment of these topics.
2. Bright, John. *The Authority of the Old Testament.* Nashville, Tenn.: Abingdon, 1967. A wrestling with the interpretation of the Old Testament and its study from a Christian perspective.
3. Wenger, J. C. *God's Word Written.* Scottdale, Pa.: Herald Press, 1966. A very helpful work written from a Mennonite perspective.

IV. The following works represent sources for some of the terminology used in this work. Although used here in a different way, the reader is referred to these items for this background.
1. Hockett, Charles F. and Robert Ascher. "The Human Revolution," *Current Anthropology* 5 (1964): 135-147. They apply the term *duality* to describe the evolution of human language.
2. Polanyi, Michael. *Personal Knowledge Towards a Post-Critical Philosophy.* Chicago: University of Chicago Press, 1958. Uses the term *tacit dimension,* although in a different context.
3. Wright, Georg H. von. *Explanation and Understanding.* Ithaca, N.Y.: Cornell University Press, 1971. The term *practical inference* is used to characterize historical explanations.